Ken Melville was following a family tradition when, after qualifying in medicine in Edinburgh, he went into general practice; however he broke that tradition in 1960 when he accepted the post of Chief Medical Officer with an international construction company in Libya — initially the only British physician in a country almost the size of India!

Having been a competitor in many car rallies, including the RAC and Monte Carlo, certainly helped him to cope with the varied terrain and problems he encountered driving from camp to camp.

He spent some months in London in 1965 to study for a Diploma in Tropical Medicine, returning shortly afterwards to the desert.

The expansion of oil exploration and development in the Sahara, with the attendant increase of disease and accidents to personnel unaccustomed to desert situations, and the seeming lack of any clear-cut advice to desert travellers at that time, prompted him to write the first edition of this book. An enthusiastic artist and photographer, he has provided most of the illustrations.

After eleven years of desert living, he has now returned to Scotland, and works with the mentally handicapped.

To
K.D.M. & M.J.M.

Publisher's Note

Travel in the deserts of the world is akin to mountain climbing — there is a strict set of rules which you break at your peril, but which, observed, will yield memorable experiences of the fascination of this other silent world. Dr. Melville lays these guiding principles on the line for readers.

The first edition of Dr. Melville's book appeared in 1970, but after initial sales in Libya, went into hibernation when political problems arose. It was eventually sold in the latter part of the decade, and we, as his publishers, started to receive good reports on it from desert buffs.

These prompted us to suggest to Dr. Melville that he might make certain changes to the contents of his book so that we could bring out a new edition well suited to desert travel in the 1980's. We in turn have changed the format and general style of the book and we like to think that between publisher and author we now have a top rate reference manual for those interested in the practicalities of desert travel and survival.

Stay Alive
in the Desert

K.E.M. Melville, L R C P & S Ed.,
L R F P & S Glas., D T M & H Lon.
Former Chief Medical Officer
Arabian Bechtel Corporation

"In this desert, as on the wide sea, the voyager is frequently impeded by storms; a furious wind lifts whirling sand over a plain lacking vegetation, filling the mouth and eyes of the voyager; in this event, it is necessary to halt the journey."

Sallus (79 B.C.)

Roger Lascelles, Cartographic and Travel Publisher
3 Holland Park Mansions, 16 Holland Park Gardens, London W14 8DY   Telephone: 01-603 8489

Publication Data

Title	Stay Alive in the Desert
Typeface	Phototypeset in Compugraphic Times
Photographs	By the author and R. Casella
Printing	Kelso Graphics, Kelso, Scotland.
ISBN	0 903909 11 1
Edition	First 1970, second Mar 1981, Reprinted Mar 1987
Publisher	Roger Lascelles
	47 York Road, Brentford, Middlesex, TW8 0QP.
Copyright	Kenmure E.M. Melville

Distribution

Africa:	South Africa —	Faradawn, Box 17161, Hillbrow 2038
Americas:	Canada —	International Travel Maps & Books, P.O. Box 2290, Vancouver BC V6B 3W5.
	U.S.A. —	Hunter Publishing Inc, 155 Riverside Dr, New York NY 10024 (212) 595 8933
Asia:	Hong Kong —	The Book Society, G.P.O. Box 7804, Hong Kong 5-241901
	India —	English Book Store, 17-L Connaught Circus/P.O. Box 328, New Delhi 110 001
	Singapore —	Graham Brash Pte Ltd., 36-C Prinsep St.
Australasia	Australia —	Rex Publications, 413 Pacific Highway, Artarmon NSW 2064. 428 3566
	New Zealand —	Enquiries invited.
Europe:	Belgium —	Brussels - Peuples et Continents
	Germany —	Available through major booksellers with good foreign travel sections
	GB/Irleand —	Available through all booksellers with good foreign travel sections.
	Italy —	Libreria dell'Automobile, Milano
	Netherlands —	Nilsson & Lamm BV, Weesp
	Denmark —	Copenhagen - Arnold Busck, G.E.C. Gad, Boghallen, G.E.C. Gad
	Finland —	Helsinki — Akateeminen Kirjakauppa
	Norway —	Oslo - Arne Gimnes/J.G. Tanum
	Sweden —	Stockholm/Esselte, Akademi Bokhandel, Fritzes, Hedengrens. Gothenburg/Gumperts, Esselte Lund/Gleerupska
	Switzerland —	Basel/Bider: Berne/Atlas; Geneve/Artou; Lausanne/Artou: Zurich/Travel Bookshop

Contents

Foreword

It is a basic part of man's nature to be curious about the unknown, which is as it should be, for without this curiosity there would be neither knowledge nor progress. Today, more than ever before, man is venturing into the deserts of the world, searching for oil, for antiquities, for knowledge — even self-knowledge. Working or travelling in the desert is a more rewarding experience for some than for others; like life anywhere, desert living is largely what one makes it.

With modern vehicles, desert travel is becoming progressively more simple, even relatively safe; however, the traveller who does not treat the desert with respect, or who relaxes his care and vigilance for an instant, is liable to find himself in grave trouble or possibly extreme danger.

This book has been prepared in the hope that it may be of guidance to those who are planning to spend some time in the desert; it is intended to show the more obvious pitfalls to be avoided, to answer some of the questions most frequently asked, and to dispel a little of the fear of the unknown which is one of man's most natural reactions.

To those who are venturing into the desert for the first time, I can guarantee an interesting experience, and to all desert travellers I wish a happy and trouble-free journey.

1. Introduction to the Desert

The desert always gives the illusion of eternal changelessness; but this *is* only an illusion — in reality it is altering all the time due to the subtle and perpetual interchange of sand and wind.

It is a world of contrasts, a world to which almost any description may be applied at some time or another — calm, violent, romantic, terrifying, drab, colourful, gentle, cruel, stifling, freezing. Man is seldom unaffected by this sense of contrast; the peace and solitude which he welcomes can easily become despair and loneliness when things go wrong.

This is the world of the desert, the land into which we are going to venture; it is a land which rapidly brings us face to face with the fundamental question of origin — How did it begin? Was it always a desert? What, in fact, **is** a desert?

Large and numerous collections of petrified wood, arrowheads, tombs, rock-carvings and fossils all combine to give us direct evidence that an era existed when the desert was a fertile, well-populated land; however, there is still much speculation as to the actual causes of deserts. Some of these causes are known, but information as to the precise sequence of events is still lacking.

Deserts usually occur in regions where the prevailing winds have to cross bordering mountains, on which they deposit their moisture and become extremely dry. The sub-tropical belts are the areas in which most of the deserts are to be found, mainly because the hot air rising from the tropics cools and drops its moisture, becoming dry; it is then deflected to the sub-tropical areas where it descends and absorbs any available moisture as it becomes warmer, thus diminishing the rainfall. Due to lack of rain, vegetation becomes scarce and is rapidly utilised, and once the roots have gone there is nothing left to bind the soil together. This lack of vegetation lays bare the land to the wind and sun, so that the elemental rock and sand features of a desert become predominant.

Man also plays his part in the creation of deserts by over-grazing in vulnerable areas, contributing to the destruction of the root system. However he is at last realising his errors and making efforts to restore the balance by dune fixation, so if you come across any area in which dunes seem to have a regular pattern of vegetation it is important to do nothing to disturb them.

The favourite romantic picture of a desert as a land of golden sand dunes does exist, but accounts for probably as little as 10-15% of the desert surface; for the rest, the desert is made up of an infinite variety of surfaces.

By definition, a desert is an area in which the mean annual precipitation is less than 25 cms (10 ins); it is an area of sparse or absent vegetation and of very low population density. 5% of the world's total land surface is extremely arid, over 30% is semi-arid. The Sahara alone is equal in size to the combined areas of Britain, France and Germany.

The principal types of true desert surface you will meet are—

Pavement Desert
This is caused by strong winds blowing most of the sand off vast areas of desert, leaving an interlocking mosaic of gravel, pebbles or boulders, known as 'Serir' in Libya, 'Reg' in the Sahara and 'Gibber Plain' in Australia. This type of surface usually gives very fast and easy motoring - 'good going' - and is very different from

Hammada
This is an extensive area of very uneven and rocky terrain over which driving is a slow and exhausting business, great care being needed to minimise damage to tyres; it is on this type of surface that your sump guards will prove their worth!

Erg (Sand Sea)
Ergs are large areas comprising actively shifting sand dunes or sand sheets or both together. The sand is very loose which makes it difficult to drive on. Dunes can be over 175 metres in height, and vary in shape according to the prevailing winds:

Crescent-shaped (*Barchan*) *dunes* occur where sand is relatively scarce, and are formed initially by the wind piling sand against an obstruction such as a small bush;

Star-shaped dunes form in similar areas but where the wind direction is constantly altering;

Ridges of transverse dunes occur when moderate winds move light sand in a sort of wash-board effect, and in such areas stronger gusts of wind cut long troughs transversely, piling the sand into occasional *longitudinal dunes.*

8

Serir — Very good going!

Erg (Sand sea) soft and unpredictable going.

9

Two examples of sand erosion, which have left grotesquely distorted Pediments.

Dunes — always on the move and liable to slippage.

Escarpment — an obvious hazard if driving at night.

Fesh-Fesh

This is a mixture of dust and gypsum which is covered by a thin crust, and on which driving is feasible with light vehicles travelling fast; but should you break through the crust the going becomes very difficult as the powdered mixture beneath is as fine as talcum powder which, as well as getting you bogged down, has a great affinity for the distributor! (This is where your points file is invaluable.)

Salt Flats and Playas

These are areas of almost perfect flatness where periodic inundations of water have soaked through the ground. Even though they look firm, great care must be taken as it is possible to become inescapably bogged down in them.

Yardang

Large masses of soft rock surfaces which have been grooved and pitted by wind erosion, leaving ridges and furrows in the same direction as the wind; mainly found in the Mojave and Turkestan deserts.

There are, of course, many other desert forms, including mesas, pediments, escarpments, pinnacles, buttes, wadis and oases; the list is enormous and the classification confused, but they all have their own special beauty and share the common feature of desolation.

It should be realised that the peoples of the desert, and the desert border towns, have their own customs, taboos and philosophies which most probably are very different from our own; their views and ways of life must be respected to the fullest extent if their help and co-operation, without which troubles will certainly multiply, are to be obtained. If one is pleasant, non-arrogant and relaxed, they will respond in like fashion; but woe betide the traveller who shows, even to the least extent, that to him they appear inferior. He will receive what he has asked for — non-co-operation.

It is wise, as well as being the basis of common good manners, to learn as much as you can of the habits and customs of those whose countries it is intended to visit. For example, to many Muslims it is a grave offence to sit in a manner which shows the soles of the shoes, and an even greater one to offer food, cigarettes or even shake hands with the left hand, which is by custom the hand used for less hygienic purposes. (I have never been able to discover how a left-handed Muslim gets on!) In many Muslim countries, alcohol, ham and pork products are banned, and western women's clothing is expected to conform to high standards of decorum. In very many countries, time does not have the same degree of urgency as in the West .... Anyone who does not know these facts in advance is therefore liable to become frustrated and angry when he encounters avoidable problems, as well as inadvertently insulting his hosts; this will help neither himself nor future expeditions. Patience is a virtue - Impatience will be disastrous.

2. The Vehicle

Choice and Preparation

The success or failure of any desert trip obviously will depend on the vehicle getting you to your destination, so it follows that care must be exercised in choosing the right type of vehicle and having it properly equipped in order to reduce the chances of failure to a minimum. Remember the maxim 'if it can go wrong, it will — and always at the most inconvenient time'. This applies in the desert at least as much as anywhere else.

If you are going to be driving in the desert off roads or beaten tracks, then you must have a vehicle equipped with optional 4-wheel drive, even though some of the early desert explorations were carried out in Model T Fords, with what difficulties one can only imagine.

Although you will find that most of your travelling can be done in 2-wheel drive, without power available to all four wheels you will be certain to get 'bogged down' frequently, and getting such a vehicle unstuck is a weary and exhausting business, as well as being expensive in terms of petrol and sweat. A 2-wheel drive vehicle can, certainly, be fitted with a limited-slip differential which does improve matters, but in the long run the preference must be for 4-wheel drive. Specially useful are those vehicles in which the change into 4-wheel drive can be made without having to stop.

The ideal vehicle for desert travel is one which has proved itself as regards dependability and toughness. It should be non-automatic, have good ground clearance and plenty of space for all the extra equipment, water and fuel that you will be obliged to carry with you; there should also be space for an additional spare wheel since desert travel puts considerable extra strain on the tyres. Electrical fuel pumps are better than the mechanical variety which tend to give trouble in hot climates. The electrical system should be 12-volt, and the engine should be water-cooled. The speedometer for preference should be marked in Kilometres per hour and it is an advantage to have a 'trip' odometer which can be reset at the beginning of each journey. An ammeter and gauges for water-temperature, oil pressure and fuel are also 'musts'.

The vehicle itself should be in good condition and if it is intended to do a large amount of desert travel with it then ideally it should not be more than 2 years old; vehicles older than this tend to suffer from a multiplicity of problems which, though minor in an urban situation, can be disastrous in the emptiness of the desert; it is asking for trouble to start out in a vehicle of doubtful or uncertain condition, or one which has been roughly or carelessly used. If you are in any doubt at all about its condition, then it is cheaper in the long run to spend a relatively small amount of money and get it thoroughly and expertly examined before committing yourself.

Compass
If you are going to fit a compass to the vehicle, make quite certain it is adjusted to the car's magnetic field, otherwise it will be very misleading. If you will be doing much of your driving over little-known areas or away from well-used tracks, then it is well worth buying a good, adjustable instrument and having it firmly mounted; such a compass will probably cost you something less than £100. However, the cheaper, non-adjustable ones can be useful **provided** they are mounted in the position in which their readings are most accurate, rather than where they look best!

To set the instrument in the best position, point the vehicle due North, and then move the compass around the cab until you find a spot where it registers due North. Fix the compass there and then point the vehicle South, East and West, checking that it is still registering accurately. Make a note of any error factor and stick it below the compass.

Together with this type of compass, however, it will also be necessary to have a good prismatic compass for taking bearings when you wish to check your position against a landmark, but this one must never be used inside the vehicle; it is important to get well away from the magnetic influence of the vehicle before taking a reading. (For more detailed information on compass errors see page 115).

Wheels
Ideally, the wheels should be the largest possible for the make and model of vehicle, bearing in mind that suitable desert tyres must be available for them. Larger wheels and tyres increase the efficiency of travel over sand, and have a slight advantage in reducing the frequency of becoming bogged down.

Tyres

Never try to economise on tyres; in desert conditions they are going to be subjected to far more than the usual amount of strain owing to the heat, the abrasive and bruising effects of sand and rock surfaces, and also to the periodic running in an under-inflated state for extra traction. Tyres which are old, are of unsuitable types, or are in poor condition must be scrapped ruthlessly and new sets purchased. I consider it essential, when preparing for a lengthy desert trip, to contact the better-known tyre companies for advice; you will find them extremely co-operative and helpful, and their advice is well worth taking seriously.

Tyre technology has now advanced so far that many 'standard' types of tyre are suitable for desert use, but if it seems likely that you will be doing much driving in areas of predominantly soft sand, it is worthwhile considering using one of the special 'sand-type' tyres which are designed to operate at the low pressures advisable in such conditions.

It might be thought that the modern 'run-flat' tyres (tyres upon which you may continue to run even though they are flat) would be a good idea for desert travel. However, this is not necessarily the case, and as there are several types of 'run-flat' tyres currently available it is strongly recommended that you consult the particular manufacturers before finally committing yourself.

Deflation

If you are not using special sand-tyres and you get into an area of soft sand, you will find that you get much better traction if you let the air out of the tyres until they bulge, as this increases the area of the bearing surface in contact with the sand and hence gives you more grip:

 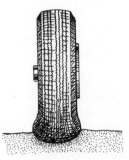

It is almost impossible to estimate the degree of bulge if you deflate the tyres when already stuck in soft sand (unless you know the pressure you want and control the deflation with a pressure gauge). Deflation otherwise should be done in advance, while still on hard ground and you can see the amount of bulge. Deflation, however, inevitably increases the fuel consumption to an even greater extent, and remember that running with deflated tyres on sand increases their temperature even more, so keep your speed down to a reasonable level, regardless of the temptation to go faster.

For desert travel, tyres must have inner tubes, rather than being tubeless; the reason is that if you deflate a tubeless tyre too much the seal between rim and tyre will be broken and the tyre will become completely flat. It is impossible to reflate a tubeless tyre with a foot-pump or an engine pump; a high pressure pump is essential, and these have a regrettable tendency to be scarce in the desert!

In the case of vehicles with dual wheels, great care must be taken not to deflate to the extent that the bulges touch each other; if they do touch, even intermittently, the friction will soon ruin both of them:

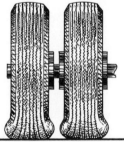

Equipment
What extra equipment you take with you will obviously depend on the type and length of your proposed trip, the space you have available, and also on the reasons for the trip. The following list of suggestions should be used as a guide only; not all of the items are essential, and there will almost certainly be others which you will wish to add, subject always to the over-riding consideration of weight. The final weight of your laden vehicle, with a full load of equipment, food, fuel, water and passengers MUST be **within** the maker's specification, otherwise you are going to find yourself in serious mechanical trouble very early on, quite apart from the increasing frequency of becoming bogged down.

Suggested Extras

1. Extras Fitted to Vehicle.

Double Roof: e.g. 'Sun Roof' as fitted to some desert and tropical vehicles; this consists of an extra, false, roof fixed on top of the existing one, so that an air space is present between the two; it definitely reduces the temperature inside the cab by several degrees. For maximum cooling effect it should be painted glossy white on the upper surface.

False Roof

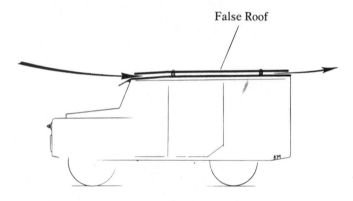

Electrical Fuel Pump: if not already fitted.

Extra Fuel Tank:, or else supporting brackets for carrying extra fuel in metal Jerrycans. Remember, with (a) much high-revving, low-gear driving, (b) the use of 4-wheel drive, (c) increased resistance of sand and (d) lower tyre pressures, your fuel consumption will be much greater than when driving on a paved surface — estimate *at least half as much again* for desert driving.

Fire Extinguisher: mounted in a convenient position **in the cab** where you can grab it quickly — not, as I have once seen, within the engine compartment "because that is where a fire is most likely to occur"!

Guards: It is well worth while having protective plates of heavy-gauge metal welded below both sump and fuel tank; much of the desert is very rocky and uneven, and a holed sump or fuel tank is one of the avoidable disasters.

Lag the Fuel Lines: with fire-proof material at any points where they pass near the exhaust manifold; this helps to stop fuel vaporising problems due to excess heat.

Seat Belts: apart from the safety factor, these will make your journey a great deal more comfortable on the rough stretches. Seat belts should be of the cross-over, rather than lap-strap, type and must, of course, be properly fitted to the frame of the vehicle, not the seat.

Seats: (hardly an extra, but included here for convenience). Ideally, seats should be fabric-covered rather than covered with leather or plastic, both of which can get uncomfortably hot — I have actually been burned by a 'leather' seat while wearing shorts! Back rests are also very useful in allowing air circulation — it is very uncomfortable driving while stuck to your seat-back! (If possible, get into the habit of tipping the seats forward whenever you leave the vehicle; again, this will help to prevent them becoming too hot).   Similarly, a steering-wheel 'glove' helps to prevent the wheel becoming unpleasantly hot if the vehicle has been left standing in the sun for any length of time.

Spare Wheels (Two!): with appropriate tyres.

Sun Visors: external or internal, if not already fitted; otherwise anti-glare strips to fit on the top of the windscreen, and which may be obtained in blue or green.   (If you wish, they may be printed with your name, a message, or even an advertisement!)

Towing Hooks: front and rear.

Trip Odometer: if not already fitted.

Water Tanks: you cannot carry too much water! (Note: plastic water bottles easily become punctured by vehicle movement and therefore should not be used. Metal containers, or else the heavy-duty polythene military type Jerrycans, are preferable, and they have the additional advantage that they can be lashed down to prevent too much movement.)

Windscreen Washers, if not already fitted.

2. Tools

Full set of Standard Tools as supplied with the vehicle.

Adjustable Spanners ('Crescent Wrenches').

'Mole' Spanner

Set of Feeler Gauges

Points File

Large, half-round, Metal File

Tyre-pressure Gauge

Tyre Pump, foot- or engine-operated. (The latter is preferable as the foot-operated types use up quite a lot of energy, hence increased sweating and therefore thirst).

2 Tyre Levers

Tyre Valve-key

Strong Hydraulic Jack, with large base-plate, or else exhaust-inflated 'Easylift' air jack ('Bull-Bag').

Strong Wheel-nut Wrench - i.e. one to which extra leverage can be added safely in the event of the nuts being found to be 'locked'.

3. Repair Kits

Carburettor Repair kit

Fuel Pump Repir kit

Water Pump Repair kit

Clutch and Brake (Master and Slave Cylinder) Repair kits

With complicated electrical equipment, it is often better to buy new — or at least 'guaranteed reconditioned' — equipment rather than repair kits; if you do this, then it is wiser to have the new equipment fitted prior to the start of your trip, and take the old parts along as spares, rather than vice versa. Certainly the battery should be replaced by a new one if it is approaching the two year old mark; even though modern car batteries are very good, they have a great deal more electrical equipment to cope with than they did in the past, and it is my experience that when they **do** fail, they do it **very** rapidly, with little or no warning.

For this reason also, it is worth while parking the vehicle on the **top** of any irregularities in the ground surface, or the top of a dune if you are in dune country; even with a new battery, it is not unknown to settle down for the night having forgotten to switch off the radio or interior lights, and a push-start on level sand is **not** to be recommended!

4. Spare Parts

Coil

Condenser (capacitor)

Set of new Spark Plugs

Set of Points (unless your vehicle is fitted with electronic ignition)

Complete set of Gaskets

Complete set of Bulbs — Headlamp, Sidelamp, etc.

Set of Fuses — of the **correct** type and strength

TWO Fan Belts. (Remember, if you are stuck with a broken fan belt and no spare, then a nylon stocking, or tights, will make an excellent substitute!)

Can of Engine Oil

Can of Brake Fluid

Can of Liquid Radiator Solder

Cans of Lubricating Oil and Penetrating Oil

2 extra Windscreen Wiper Blades

Emergency Plastic Windscreen

Spare Radiator Water-hoses, with Jubilee clips to fit

Cables — Brake, Clutch and Accelerator

It may even be worthwhile adding a spare Distributor Cap to the list, especially if the car is not new; I have had 3 crack in two different cars within 1½ years — with fairly disastrous results!

5. Miscellaneous Equipment

Food and Cooking Equipment (see page 123).

Medical Supplies (see page 125).

Set of Jump Leads (for starting a vehicle with a flat battery from the battery of another vehicle).

Roll of Heavy Duty Plastic Electrical Tape — useful for many minor repairs, even leaking water-hose.

Reel-Lamp; this is a practical and useful lamp on a 3.65 metre cable which plugs into the cigar socket and has a magnetic base.

Electric Torch with spare Batteries and Bulbs.

Fuse-wire — assorted values.

Matches, Cigarette Lighter, Flints, Fuel, etc.

Aerosol Fly-sprays.

2 pieces of Canvas Belting (25cms x 2m approx) — for getting 'unstuck', with approx 3m strong cord attached.

2 multi-ply Wooden Blocks (2-3cm x 30cm x 50cm approx) — for placing beneath the base plate of the jack in soft sand.

Spade or Shovel.

Strong Tow-Rope, preferably polypropylene, not less than 4 metres in length excluding the hooks.

Stainless Steel Vacuum Flask for drinking water; although expensive, it will stand up to a fantastic amount of ill-treatment.

'Swiss Army' Type Pocket Knife — incredibly useful for many small jobs, and always to hand.

Workshop Repair Manual for the model of vehicle concerned.

2 Spare Ignition Keys — 1 to be hidden on the exterior of the vehicle.

Sheet of Polythene, approx 2 x 2 metres (see page 43)

Hand Lens (Magnifying glass).

Assortment of Nuts and Bolts.

Assortment of Self-tapping Screws.

Any Maps of the area on which you can lay your hands!

NOTE: As much as possible of the extra equipment which you acquire for your trip should be under strong lock and key.

Last Minute Vehicle Checks

If you have done much flying you will know that, no matter how urgent the flight, no pilot will ever take off before he has done his routine series of checks; true, he may speed up the process sometimes, but he will always do them. In normal everyday driving you can afford to jump into your car, start the engine and drive off, as in the unlikely event of trouble there are generally plenty of garages, or people with some knowledge, to help you.

However, desert driving should be treated as a flight — if things go wrong you are on your own. It is common sense to spend a couple of minutes before starting off to make sure that all is as it should be. You can often save yourself considerable embarrassment, not to mention danger, and you can save others time and worry. Make it a firm rule to **check for yourself** — do not take anyone else's word for it that the oil or water levels are alright — they may have leaked since then, or he may have been checking a different vehicle.

So, before you start up, check the engine oil-level, fan-belt, radiator water, and have a look to make sure the battery is not dry; check the tyre pressures (not forgetting the spares) and then make sure that you have all the equipment you may need for your trip — tools, jack, compass, tyre-pump, etc. — all things that might have been 'borrowed' when your back was turned.

Next, set your trip-odometer to zero. Make sure that you have your drinking water, food, can-opener and all that you will need personally, and that everything that can be tied down and made secure from vibration is so. Finally, start the engine and check that you have enough fuel, that the dynamo or alternator is charging, that the oil-pressure is normal, that the engine is not overheating and that it sounds normal. If all IS normal, then at last you are in a position to 'check out', wave goodbye to your friends and start off — preferably in the right direction. (A friend of mine did all his checks and then drove off due south instead of north as he had intended. He had driven almost 70 kms before he realised his mistake!) You must do these checks EVERY time you set off into the desert.

At this moment you're possibly saying to yourself 'Life's too short to bother with all this'; but if you don't do these checks it may be a lot shorter! Always treat the desert with respect.

Selection of World War II mines.

Camels

Should you choose to travel by camel, I strongly recommend that you look elsewhere than this book for information about them, possibly starting at the local zoo. I have once been on a camel, and it was a matter of considerable doubt as to whether the camel or I disliked the experience more.

This does not diminish my admiration for it; as an example of adaptation to its environment, the camel must surely reign supreme amongst mammals. With its small round ears, slit nostrils, long-lashed eyes, long legs and padded broad feet, to say nothing of its ability to travel 4-5 days without water, it is ideally equipped for the desert.

If you are determined to use camels, however, you must decide how many you need, and whether to buy or hire, remembering that to buy a single camel will probably cost around £400. (I regret I have no knowledge of the re-sale value of a "never-been-raced-one-careful-user" camel!) It is also worth remembering that the harder the bargain you strike, the cheaper will be the price and the greater the respect in which you will be held by the dealer.

Bear in mind that you can only plan on a distance of 20 miles per day, so that your trip will obviously take longer than by a vehicle; I was once told that after the first 3 days you will have a very sore bottom indeed, so in planning your itinerary, the enforced stop for the 4th and 5th days should be taken into account. Against this, camels can go where vehicles cannot.

Lastly, if like me, you are not an experienced camel driver, you will need to employ a camel-handler to feed, load and control them.

3. En Route in the Desert

Explosives—A Word of Warning

In the deserts of North Africa there are still many grim reminders of World War II to be found in the shape of unexploded bombs, mines, mortar shells, grenades and other forms of explosives.

Although large mine fields have for the most part been cleared, and although the passage of more than thirty-five years has rendered many of those that are left harmless, remember that explosives often have a tendency to become more unstable in time and that it does not always need a detonator to set them off; this applies specially in the extreme dryness of desert regions.

Therefore, if you do find any abandoned ammunition dumps, leave them strictly alone and resist the temptation to take along a 'souvenir'. Even today, tragedies still occur when children find an old grenade and start to play with it.

Unhappily, this warning now also applies to the large number of deserts in the Middle East which have recently been theatres of modern warfare.

Generally, however, you will be perfectly safe if you stick to well-travelled routes, or at least keep well away from any suspicious-looking objects in sand. Take special care when you are driving in the vicinity of old abandoned wartime airstrips — there are often small forgotten piles of ammunition and mines to be found near them, and the approaches to the strips were often mined, and may still be dangerous.

KM

Getting Stuck — How not to!

Remember, it is always easier to avoid getting stuck in the first place than it is to get out when you are, and it is well worth while seeing how we can avoid this aggravating mishap. Becoming bogged down in soft sand is generally the result of the sand being softer than was originally thought. How can we steer clear of sand which is too soft, and how can we avoid getting into this type of trouble?

1 Travel Early or Late
In the early morning, sand is cooler and more moist, therefore closer packed and firmer; the result is that the going is much better. Also, early morning or late afternoon are the best times for travelling as the low position of the sun gives plenty of shadows which show up the textures of the sand; at noon, all detail is generally lost and the sun-glare can be so great that no idea of distance can be gained; in conditions like this, many cars and trucks have driven into a near-vertical sand slope wrecking the car — and sometimes the unfortunate driver, who could see no slope and thought he was still driving along a good level stretch. **Under no circumstances, however, should you ever set out in a sandstorm or at night.** This is invariably highly dangerous in both cases, and you will be very likely to damage the vehicle considerably, if not yourself.

2 Surface Appearances

Beware of patches showing a sudden change in appearance and consistency, e.g. hard dark surface changing suddenly into soft brown. Ruts left by the wheels of other vehicles give a lot of information — look for sudden deepening and widening, a sure sign of the sand becoming softer; blurring of the edges and loss of detail of the tread can indicate an old track, but if all the tracks are similar in this appearance it is more likely to mean that the sand is soft; a 'chewed-up' appearance in which all detail has disappeared always indicates trouble and should be avoided. Salt flats near the coast can sometimes look deceptively smooth and hard whereas they may in fact be extremely soft and difficult to get out of.

Soft patch on good going.

3 Engine Speed

Never 'rev' the engine too much unless you are already moving fairly rapidly; high revs when you are moving slowly in soft sand will dig you in deeply; in the same conditions — moving slowly and with difficulty in soft sand — if the vehicle starts to jerk, then stop at once; if you don't, the chances are that you will dig in more than you will move forward, until you are brought to an abrupt halt anyway. If the surface is uncertain, keep going at a pace brisk enough to carry you through small, unexpected soft patches, but not so fast that you may cause damage if you hit a sudden hidden obstruction. If sand conditions are gradually slowing you down and the appearances are that the sand is still getting softer, then change down to a lower gear **before you think you need to** — in other words, while you still have plenty of momentum. Alternatively, change your direction and try to drive round the soft and difficult patch, not forgetting to make a note of your new compass heading and the mileage reading on the odometer so that you can revert to your original heading when the surface improves.

Good going.

4   Transverse Ruts

Whenever you start to cross a series of tracks running at right-angles to you, slow down and watch out, because in the middle of these is often at least one main track which is very deep; if you hit this track at any speed, you will be very likely to damage your front suspension severely. If you see this kind of track, cross it very gently at an angle.

Deep ruts — very dangerous if you hit them at right-angles.

5 Sand Dunes

It is important to remember that sand is not a constant medium, but one which is perpetually shifting and changing; therefore be careful not to fall into the trap of assuming that the surface will be the same as it was the last time you travelled over it. Even a track which you travelled over the previous day must not be taken for granted; this applies particularly to tracks leading over sand dunes as sometimes wind action may cause the whole of one side of a dune to collapse, forming a steep 'Slip-Face'.

This .... can become .... This

Slip-faces are naturally extremely dangerous to drivers; you may be driving over a well-known dune only to find when you reach the top that there is no gentle slope down the other side, only a steep, precipitous drop, and by this time it may be too late to stop — and remember, in the Sahara some dunes can be as much as 150 metres (500 ft) high! There have been many deaths in the desert due to excessive speed over the top of a dune which has 'slipped'. So, when you are driving over dunes, even though you will probably have to really charge them at full speed to get up them, **you must always slow down at the crest and be prepared for an emergency stop.**

Be prepared to stop on the crest of a dune.

Like many others, I have once gone over a slip-face, and also like many others I decided that once was more than enough! If you should be unfortunate enough to go over the top of an unexpected slip-face, and find yourself plunging headlong down a slope much steeper than you had anticipated, then the only thing to do is to fight against your instincts and **accelerate hard;** this tends to bring the rear end of the vehicle down, and you will then just have to charge down the slope, doing your best to stay upright.

If you brake instead of accelerating then you will certainly dig the front end of the vehicle into the sand and may very easily find yourself somersaulting down to the bottom. However if you go over the edge of the slip-face at an angle rather than at right angles it is almost certain that the vehicle will roll over sideways, and your only possible action is to try to prevent this by turning your wheels to point downhill; if you are lucky, you may then be able to 'ride it out'.

Another reason why you should be ready to stop at once on the top of a dune is that there just might be another vehicle coming up the other side in the same line as you; strange though it may seem, there **have** been head-on collisions in the desert before now in exactly these circumstances.

Lastly, if you are in an area which you have not visited recently, or indeed, at all, then stop on the top and have a good look round at the other dunes before descending. It is possible that you might be on the edge of a 'ring-dune' and if you once go down into the hollow, you could well find the sides too steep to allow you to drive out. Lowering a dune by hand is not really to be recommended!

If you fail to get up a dune and there appears to be no way round it, then back off a really good distance (on to level ground if possible), let your tyres down further if you can (check with tyre gauge) and charge at it as hard as you can, remembering to engage your lower gears before you would normally think of doing so, and also remembering to slow down or stop on the crest; you should, of course, be using drive on all 4 wheels.

Driving over sand dunes can be very exhilarating and good fun, but, like everything else in the desert, it must be treated with respect.

6 Oil Roads

With the amount of oil exploration and development going on all over the world at present, there are plenty of 'oil roads' to be found. These are roads made by grading the desert surface and then layering with crude oil which becomes compacted to form a hard and — for a time — smooth surface. There are dangers to be noted with these roads, however. They are often badly broken and irregular, specially on each side of a rise, and can cause severe damage to the suspension. They are **extremely dangerous** when wet, being just as slippery as ice; this is often the case in early morning when there may be condensation on them. Frequently they are narrow, so that to pass another vehicle you may have to get two wheels off into the sand, in which case you must be prepared for a sudden pull to the side as your wheels meet the increased resistance of the sand, otherwise you can easily find yourself spinning right off the road.

Oil rig in the desert.

7 Sandstorms

In actual fact, there are two varieties — sandstorms proper and dust-storms. The latter are the result of fine dust being lifted into the air by prolonged winds, to a height of many miles, and are most uncomfortable, making the very act of breathing quite an adventure! Generally they die out slowly as the light dust particles settle only very gently.

Sandstorms however occur when the wind is strong enough to lift the heavier grains of sand off the desert surface, and they rarely rise above 5 metres — hence the weird 'mushroom' carvings of buttes which are often seen. Unfortunately, however, man is not 5 metres tall, so sandstorms are as uncomfortable for him as dust-storms, or even more so.

It is essential to wrap up against the abrasive effect of the sand — and let there be no doubt that it is abrasive! Once, whilst driving in the desert, I ran into a very severe sandstorm; horizontal visibility was immediately blotted out (though I was able to see blue sky above) so of course I had to stop at once; after 25 minutes of noise and vibration, the storm passed almost as suddenly as it had arisen. I found that my car had been turned through 90° and was standing across the road, that its front had been stripped clean of all paint right down to the gleaming metal, and that the windscreen and headlamp glasses were sand-blasted and useless. It served me right for not having turned at the beginning to expose the rear of the car to the wind. There is only one piece of advice that I can give you about driving in sand-storms or dust-storms — DON'T!

8 Final word

Don't forget to keep an eye from time to time on your mileage, compass, fuel, ammeter and water temperature gauges.

How to get out when Stuck in Soft Sand

1 Stop at Once
Do not under any circumstances race the engine to try to get the vehicle out; you will only dig yourself in deeply very rapidly.

2 Engage your lowest gear in 4-wheel drive and, without excessive engine speed, try to drive out gently. Don't forget that in many vehicles the ratio of reverse gear is lower than that of first and you can sometimes reverse out of a situation where you cannot go forward.

3 If this does not work, get out and check the tyre pressures with the gauge, lowering them further if possible; clear the sand away from in front of all 4 wheels with a spade or with your hands so as to make a more gentle slope and then try (2) again.

Supposing that you have tried all this without success, you are still stuck and there is no other vehicle available to pull you out, then:

4 Jack up the vehicle using your wooden blocks as baseplates, and place something 'solid' beneath the rear wheels — sand belts if you have them, otherwise flat stones, brushwood, blankets, mats from the car interior or even the spare wheels; lower the vehicle off the jack onto your improvised road and drive off. Two points are worth remembering: **a.** Decide which way you are going to move — it is no use getting out of one lot of soft sand and driving straight into another, and yet I have seen this done more than once when all that was necessary was to go backwards rather than forwards (in which case, your 'improvised road' should be put under your front wheels). **b.** It is worth while having a long piece of strong cord (about 3 metres) tied from the vehicle to whatever you were using so that, once you have got going again, you do not have to stop to go back to collect them, only to find that you cannot start off once more without digging in again.

5 Your vehicle may be one equipped with a starting handle. If so, don't forget the old trick when stuck of taking out the sparking plugs, engaging the suitable gear, releasing the hand brake, and 'winding' the vehicle out of the place in which it is stuck.

6 Remember not to over-exert yourself if it is very hot; take it easily and do not rush, otherwise you will tire rapidly and sweat too much, and it is possible that you will need all your moisture if you are really stuck!

7   Finally, if you cannot manage to get yourself unstuck by any of the above methods, or if you have broken down beyond your ability to repair, then you will have to wait for help to come; unless you are within *easy* walking distance of the camp (not more than 5 kilometres in hot weather) DO NOT LEAVE YOUR VEHICLE.

It is not easy to find a vehicle in the desert — it is almost impossible to find a man. Never leave the vehicle unless you **know** the exact distance you are going to travel, you can **see** your destination, and the weather is cool enough to walk; if it is very hot, then wait till evening. Never try to walk if you are already thirsty and have no water left. Never try to judge the distance by eye — this is one of the most deceptive things in the desert.

A true story to show how difficult this can be: one morning I was driving across the desert to visit a new camp for the first time. The weather was hot, sunny and windless, and the going was good, enabling me to maintain an average speed of 50 m.p.h. (80 k.p.h.). I was driving on a compass bearing, keeping my eyes open for the large warehouse which I knew had been built at the camp and which would be the first visual indication that I was getting near.

Sure enough, in due course I saw a black rectangular object on the horizon ahead and drove straight towards it. At the end of 15 minutes, however, it was no bigger and though puzzled, I kept going until the 'warehouse' suddenly began to enlarge very rapidly indeed; it seemed almost to leap at me from the ground and became obvious for what it was — a blackened, rusty Jerrycan! It had been clearly visible for 17 miles, and mirage-type distortion had kept it at apparently the same size, this effect of its size lessening as my distance also lessened! Which is probably a good point to mention .....

Mirages
A mirage is an optical illusion. The most commonly recognised type is that in which, owing to refraction of light by unequal densities in the layers of air, portions of blue sky are seen as if they are on the ground, the shimmering effect making them look not unlike pools of water. You will almost certainly have seen the same effect — to a lesser extent — on roads in a hot summer at home.

Personally, I have always found this type of mirage obvious, easy to spot for what it is, and not really likely to fool anyone!

Much more intriguing is the illusion resulting from distortion of an existing object — as with the Jerrycan above. Another similar example was on an occasion when I was driving north on a Sahara road I had travelled many times before. Suddenly, ahead and to the right, I could see a large Arab town, complete with small white buildings, large white buildings, mosques and minarets. I knew there was no town there, and yet I could see it. (To my eternal regret, I had no camera with me!) Of course, when I got nearer the 'town', it disappeared and resolved into what it really was, a small escarpment, about 15 ft. (4½m) high, with several white blocks of stone in the vertical, reddish surface. Although I travelled the same road many times after, in what to me were indentical atmospheric conditions, I never again experienced this remarkable effect.

Getting Lost

To the traveller, the desert always seems to be vast and empty, and so it is; but never is it quite so vast or quite so empty as it is at the moment when the suspicion that you may be lost becomes a certainty.

In almost every case, getting lost while driving in the desert is the result of sheer carelessness followed by panicky and muddled thinking. If you do manage to get lost, not only is it extremely dangerous to you yourself but also to all those who have to go and look for you, possibly in unsuitable weather conditions; it can also prove to be appallingly expensive.

Some time ago, four men got lost in the Libyan desert in circumstances which were careless in the extreme; they left their camp in a 2-wheel drive family car to drive an easy 15 kilometres to another camp which, on a clear day, was clearly visible; however, they set off in a sandstorm, without water, or food, and with a faulty compass. They realised they were lost and, after much aimless wandering, eventually they stopped.

Two aircraft spent the whole of the next day searching for them without success, and by the following day, when another sandstorm was blowing, no fewer than five aircraft were searching. By setting fire to the spare tyre they attracted the attention of the pilot of one of the planes, and eventually were rescued from their predicament two-and-a-half days after they had set out. They were **one hundred and twenty eight kilometres** from their destination!

This true story is a graphic example of one of the less commonly realised facts: **it is often the short, everyday trip that one gets careless about, rather than the long, adventurous one for the first time to a new area.** Once a journey has been done a few times, there is a real danger that the driver will treat it no more seriously than a trip round the block.

In this case, the men broke several rules, and then, even when they realised they were lost, broke a further one by not stopping at once, otherwise they would never have managed to get as far away from their destination as 128 kilometres.

To make desert travel as safe as possible, it is necessary for the traveller to have some concrete plan of action ready in his own mind in case he does get lost. **The absolutely fatal thing is to rely on instinct to show you the way** — instinct will rapidly have you driving round in circles, hopelessly confused.

How then are you going to tackle the problem if you think you may be lost?

First of all, obvious though it may sound, there comes a time when you must decide that you ARE lost; a great deal of the trouble that people get into results from their failure to accept the fact that they are lost until far too late, preferring to continue in a vague, hopeful manner rather than to stop and think.

When you finally reach this conclusion, the next thing to do is to drive out of any gully or wadi that you might be in and aim for the nearest high ground or, if there is no high ground, for the nearest flat, open stretch of desert where you must then stop; it is easier for searchers to spot you there than if you are hidden in a depression.

Next, sit back calmly, take plenty of time, and try to work out where you are. Work out how far you have travelled and in which direction, and if you have a map with you, plot your position to scale on it, and see how far it is from where you make your present position to the nearest point of civilisation or to your intended destination.

If you can manage to do this it means, of course, that you are not really lost at all! Work out how much fuel you have got left and how far it will take you; if you have not enough left to reach your destination, can you follow your own tracks back to your point of origin? If you have travelled over much stony ground the tracks will probably be invisible, but if you have been driving for the most part over sand then you ought to be able to follow them — but, have you enough fuel to do so? Were there any familiar landmarks or well-travelled tracks to which you can find your way back? How long will it be before you are missed and a search begins? All of this is obvious common-sense, but these questions must be settled in your own mind before you decide on your next moves.

Direction Finding

However, suppose you have neither a map nor a compass, but, although you do not know where you are, you do know that if you travel, say, due West you will eventually hit a track which will take you back to civilisation; how, then, do you decide in which direction West lies? Obviously it becomes necessary to locate the points of the compass, and there are several simple methods of doing this.

If you have a watch with you which is reasonably accurate, point the hour hand towards the sun and note the angle between the hour hand and 12 o'clock; if you then bisect this angle, the resulting line points approximately South if you are in the Northern hemisphere and approximately North in the Southern hemisphere.

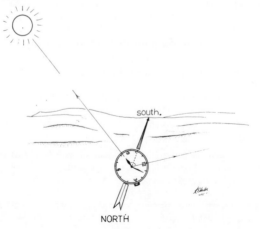

If you have no watch, put a **vertical** stick in the sand and watch the shadow it casts, marking the end of the shadow every half-hour or so. (Any simple home-made plumb-line will enable you to make sure the stick is vertical). The shortest shadow will occur at noon and when the sun is due South; (if you have a watch which had stopped, you can now calculate the time enough to be able to set it approximately) therefore, a line from the base of the stick, along the shortest shadow will be pointing due North.

(Again, in the Southern Hemisphere, substitute 'North' for 'South' and 'South' for 'North'.)

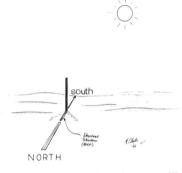

south

Shortest Shadow (Noon)

NORTH

If you know the direction of the prevailing wind, **or the direction of the last strong wind,** look around for small bushes or shrubs; you will find that the sand tends to pile up in a line behind the bush away from the wind, so by looking at the direction of this sand you can orientate yourself quite easily:-

If you know that somewhere nearby is the coast, or a large lake, look at the colour of the sky just above the horizon; you will find that the slightly pinkish tinge above the desert changes abruptly to a decidedly bluish tinge above the water, and you can pinpoint the position of the shore-line very accurately.

At night, man has turned to the stars to find his way for centuries, and continues to do so even in the Space Age. It is reassuring to find an object as constant in its wanderings as Polaris, the 'Pole Star', which never moves more than one degree from true North. This star, as nearly everyone must know, is easily found; first of all it is necessary to locate the 'Plough' or 'Big Dipper', then take a line from the two 'pointers' as shown below; this line guides you almost directly to Polaris.

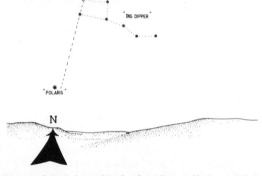

Another useful night guide is the 'Constellation of Orion', a group of seven stars, the three in the middle being known as the 'Belt of Orion'. The top star of the Belt of Orion will always rise due East and set due West, no matter where you are on the surface of the earth.

belt of orion

In the Southern hemisphere, the most useful star guide is the 'Southern Cross' constellation. If the two stars forming the stem of the cross are projected a further four times the distance between them, from the foot of the cross, then the final (imaginary) point reached is in the general direction of South.

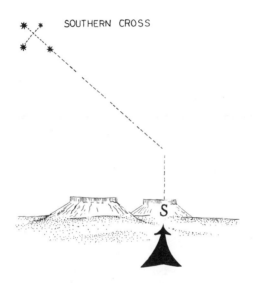

SOUTHERN CROSS

Once you have located North, South, East or West by one of these stars, don't forget to put some form of pointer towards it on the ground so that when daylight comes you will still be able to orientate yourself; also you will be able to check your compass for any suspected error.

But, let us assume that your compass is working perfectly and that when you get lost you know where North and South are, but you just don't know where **you** are. **Then you must stay with your vehicle and wait for help.** Under no circumstances should you drive any further, as the further you drive from your starting point the more difficult it is going to be to find you. 'Waiting for help', however, is by no means the idle, inactive process that it sounds; you have a lot to do!

Waiting for Help

A. Water

Water is going to be your biggest problem, so it is essential to consider it thoroughly. An active, working man in a temperature of over 100°F may need to drink up to 8, or even 12, litres of water per day. Therefore, never underestimate your requirements of water in the desert.

1. Start by checking how much water you have with you, from all sources — but remember that radiator water, if it has anti-freeze or anti-rust preparations in it, is poisonous and can quite easily prove fatal if drunk. (If it has no additives such as these it will taste unpleasant but is safe to drink.)

2. In most novels and stories of adventure where the hero is lost in the desert or adrift in an open boat, you will find that he rations his water supply very carefully, dividing it into small, infrequent sips, trying to preserve it as long as possible. **This method of consuming a water supply has been proved to be entirely wrong,** and personally I can think of few things which would drive me crazy more rapidly than to have a raging thirst and yet have to go from hour to hour, obsessed with the single thought of the next sip! In any case, very soon after you drink, you will start sweating, and if you are only having small sips you may actually sweat out more fluid than you have drunk, making a serious situation much worse.

The correct thing to do is to abstain from drinking as long as you possibly can; when your thirst can no longer be ignored, then **drink as much as you want (or as much as you have,** which-ever applies). Once you have done this, and really satisfied your thirst, you will then be able to forget about water for a while; you will find you can think more normally and can concentrate on trying to work out how you are going to escape from your predicament. More importantly, you are going to be able to function normally for a lot longer than by trying to spin out your water supply.

3. **Reduce your requirements of water** by cutting down your fluid loss:

i. Keep a thin layer of clothes on, as by doing this you will not lose so much sweat by evaporation — strange though it may seem, you will actually feel cooler by keeping a thin shirt on than you will if you take it off.

ii. Move slowly and easily, and if possible postpone any strenuous activity till the night when it is cooler and you will not sweat so much.

iii. Keep in the shade as much as you can during the day.

4. **Try to get extra supplies of water** by (a) collecting dew (b) digging (c) making a solar still.

(a) **Dew.** Remember that in the desert, dew is often deposited during the night, collecting on the metal parts and glass of a vehicle, so make preparations to salvage as much of this as possible; soak it up with cloths and wring them out into your water jug — don't forget the under surfaces will often have as much moisture as the top. Where the dew is likely to run down the sloping or vertical surfaces and be lost (e.g. windows) take the precaution of wedging a cloth at the bottom of these surfaces the previous evening so that any moisture can be wrung out the following morning. Dew also collects on stones and smooth pebbles, so collect any of these there may be in the vicinity and place them on a suitable collecting surface — hollowed-out piece of metal from the vehicle (e.g. inverted mudguard), sheet of polythene, rubber ground-sheet etc.

(b) **Digging.** There is a lot more water just beneath the surface of a desert than is generally realised, so during the cool of the night try digging for water; a likely spot is often at the base of the steep side of a sand dune or a rocky outgrowth. Any small bushes or patches of scrub may indicate the presence of water below the surface, so try digging there. Remember that animal trails may lead to a water hole, **but don't waste** too much energy following a single trail too far.

(c) **Solar Still.** Another method of collecting water is the Solar Still, which works by attracting the moisture content of the ground. Dig a hole about 1 metre across and in the bottom of it place a can, open at the top; spread your sheet of polythene (see page 22) over the hole, fixing it with stones or weights of any kind — e.g. vehicle tool kit, — on the edges; place a stone on the middle to weight it down. Available water vapour will

43

collect on the under surface of the sheeting and will run down into the can.

The process will work more efficiently if you can find some plants or shrubs to place loosely in the hole beneath the sheeting. An added refinement is to place the end of a piece of tubing in the can, the other end protruding from under the polythene sheeting on the surface. This means that you can suck the water from the can without having to disturb the still and interrupt its working. A properly constructed still will yield up to two litres of water per day, and it is worth realising that four litres should enable you to walk about 30 kms.

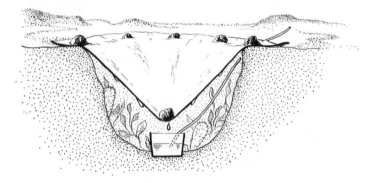

5.   Finally, it is important to boil, or treat with Halazone tablets any water you may manage to collect (other than from a solar still) — there is little use in replacing your fluid loss with water which is going to dehydrate you still further by giving you diarrhoea or making you vomit.

B. Make Preparations for Attracting Attention.

When a search plane appears, it will most likely be flying low and will soon be past if you are not prepared for it; therefore it is essential to have everything ready to attract the attention of the pilot at a moment's notice.

1. Remove the driving mirror or any other polished reflecting surface from the vehicle and keep it in some convenient place ready for immediate use when required. A flashing light will attract attention more quickly than almost anything else.

   If you remove the metal backing from the mirror and scratch a fine cross through the coating, you will find that you can then 'sight' on the plane, and by tilting the mirror back and forwards you are much more likely to be accurate in catching the eye of the pilot.

2. Nature avoids straight lines; therefore try to **create a regular pattern** of some sort, of a size big enough to be visible from the air; arrange the seats, mats, rugs, suitcases, sand-belts, wheels and any other large objects you have in a regular pattern beside the vehicle to increase its apparent size, and to attract attention by its regularity.

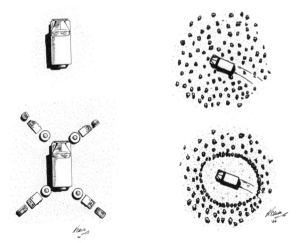

45

Keep this absolutely free from drifting sand. Other patterns can be formed by digging trenches, deep enough to throw shadows — these trenches can also be used to form words, or the letters 'S.O.S.' which are probably better as they can be read from two directions. If you have spare oil, use that to darken large areas of sand, or to write 'S.O.S.' again, but be sure to keep enough over for signal fires.

If the area in which you have decided to wait for help is sandy, then drive the vehicle round in a wide circle, the bigger the better, at least a dozen times so as to form two deep, parallel ruts, then park the vehicle in the centre.

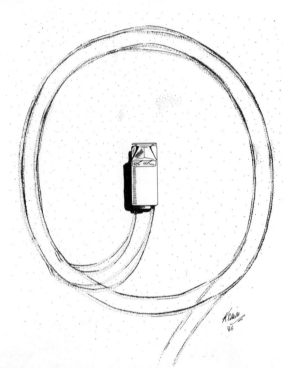

If you are in an area of scrub, uproot as many of the bushes immediately around the vehicle as you can and arrange them between the nearest ones still growing so as to form a denser ring round an open space, in the centre of which is the vehicle. (See page 45).

3. **Prepare Flare-Cans** by filling any suitable receptacles —
e.g. empty food cans, fuel drums or even cooking utensils —
with sand which is then soaked with oil from the sump or gearbox. These will burn with a dense, black smoke which on a clear
day is visible for miles. You will probably have to prime them
with petrol, in which case the lighting must be done cautiously.

You can also build a fire ready for lighting, using any easily
combustible materials you may have, and keeping in readiness
nearby engine oil, rubber mats or tyres, to be added only when
the fire is well alight; they will all burn with a dense black
smoke.

Note: Means of Ignition. Fires and Flares are obviously only of
use if you can light them, and almost certainly you will have
matches or a cigarette lighter with you. However, if you are
stranded without either of these, how are you going to start your
fire? A good piece of extra equipment to carry with you is a
normal hand-lens, in which case there is no problem; but if you
don't have this, you do have a battery and this can be utilised
quite simply to provide a flame as follows:

i.   Remove a piece of wire about 1 metre in length from behind
the dashboard.

ii.   Strip off the insulation and take out 1 strand.

iii.   Wrap it around a pencil to make it into a coil, then remove
the pencil.

iv.   Fasten one end of the wire to one pole of the vehicle battery
by twisting it around the pole.

v.   Supporting the wire by some kind of insulated material —
e.g. the pencil — touch the other end of the wire to the other
pole of the battery and hold it there firmly.

vi.   The wire will immediately glow and become red-hot, and if
you then hold a piece of paper to it, the paper will burst into
flames.

C. Food

Next, check your food supply; food is of course very important, but to nothing like the same extent as water, which is vital. You will almost certainly have a bigger water problem than a food one, even if you have hardly any food with you; a man can remain alive in the desert for many days without food, but very, very few without water. It is also worth while considering that eating — especially a diet rich in fats — is apt to increase your thirst, so be very careful if you are short of water.

Probably the best food for survival purposes is that which is most readily absorbed into the blood-stream, this being Carbohydrate (Sugar), though remember that following burns, severe vomiting and diarrhoea or injuries, the body is likely to be deficient in protein. It is not widely known that Beans, Lentils and Groundnuts are all **richer** sources of protein than meat and fish!

However, if you are stranded without food and likely to be stranded for several days, then obviously you must try to find some.

1. Look for signs of animal life — tracks, droppings, or holes in the ground which may be inhabited by animals. Remember, when you are desperate you can eat almost any animal — even rodents, lizards, birds, dogs, foxes, snakes, ants, locusts, bats, gazelles — but, where feasible, they must be skinned, gutted and cleaned in the usual way. Camel, if young, can be prepared and eaten as beef, and is very palatable; however, if old, it is better stewed. Snails are also edible, but it is better to starve them for 24 hours on sand, to dry out the slime before boiling and eating, so that they may first excrete any vegetation which they have eaten of a type which might be poisonous to you.

2. If you find signs of animal life in the vicinity, then make preparations for trapping; make slipnoose snares from the ignition wiring of the vehicle, or any other type of snare you can devise from the materials you have available, and place them on or near the tracks. You can try to smoke animals out of holes in the ground with oily, smouldering rags stuffed into the openings, and you can even try to make a catapult out of the rubber windowseals which are present on most vehicles; with this — and a little practice — you will soon be able to kill small animals.

3.   If you can find any desert plants, parts of some of these can be eaten quite safely, but avoid trying to eat any plants which produce a **milky** fluid when you cut them. All plants should be boiled before eating, and even then you should eat only a very little at a time until you are sure that they have no ill effects. 'Prickly Pear' cactus, however, is pretty safe and can be eaten raw, though it is probably better stewed. Dates, (from the date palms) are **very** nourishing with a high sugar content and if fresh have quite a good water content. (Dates keep very well and are an excellent food to buy locally and take with you into the desert).

A final note on cooking; when boiling, keep the lids of the pans on; this means that you will need much less water, which otherwise would be wasted by evaporation.

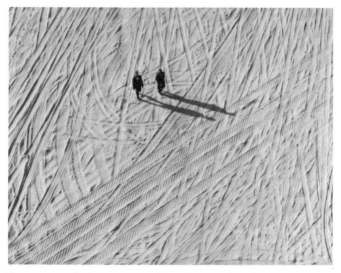

Do not try to find your way by following tracks!

D.   Landing Strip

Try to find a suitable area for a light plane to land — fairly smooth and hard — and free it of all large stones or boulders; try to indicate it with markers of some sort, such as large stones or some of the remaining objects from the vehicle — tin cans, boxes, jerry-cans, tool-box, battery, clothes, books — and if possible rig up some form of wind-sock — tie a shirt by its sleeves to any vertical pole, radio antenna, long jack-handle, etc. — or alternatively light your flare when the plane appears so that smoke will indicate wind direction. These measures will all help the pilot who, once he has spotted you, will not have to waste time and fuel trying to find a suitable place to land.

Failing all of these, you yourself can go to the end of the area you have selected for his landing, and by exaggerated vertical swings of both arms together you can indicate the strip.

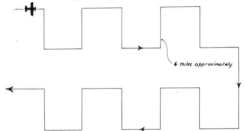

4 miles approximately

Above is a flight pattern which is commonly used by pilots who are searching in the desert areas. Remember, when in level flight a pilot very seldom sees what is on the ground for several miles in front of him as the nose of the plane obscures his vision; he usually looks out of the side windows. Therefore, if a plane is coming straight towards you, do not be too disappointed if the pilot does not seem to see you — he will soon be be turning off at right angles, and this is the moment when you should start flashing your mirror and trying to attract his attention.

Finally, when the plane has landed, do not waste your remaining energy rushing up to it; it will come to you, and in any case the pilot will be a lot fitter than you.

All these measures that you should take if you get lost mean that you will have plenty to do; they are by no means the only things — doubtless you will be able to think up many other ideas — but at least they may give you an idea or two to work on. Above all, do not panic! Your life will very probably depend on clear thinking and unhurried activity.

Engine Failure

One of the less happy experiences of desert travel arises when you are merrily driving along on a smooth, hard piece of sand, miles from anywhere, when, without warning your engine chokes, splutters and dies. All of a sudden, you become extremely small, ignorant and insignificant, and the desert becomes correspondingly large, wise and powerful!

It is to try to give some help in locating a few — by no means all — of the more common causes of engine failure that this section is included.

Engine Fails to Start

1. Battery dead, or connection loose. (Check).

2. Dirt between points in distributor. (Use File).

3. Cracked insulation on sparking-plug leads or on main lead, or disconnected main lead (Check all leads).

4. No fuel or blocked fuel lines, or air leaks in suction line from tank to pump. (Try hand pump).

Engine Starts but Soon Stops

1. Fuel shortage (see 4. above). Check flow of petrol to carburettor by disconnecting fuel inlet pipe, and either switching on ignition (electrical pump) or hand-priming (mechanical pump); if faulty, check: a. Fuel level in tank. b. Faulty pump. c. Blocked filters or pipes.
2. Check carburettor jets.

Engine Misfires

1. Low battery charge.

2. Sparking plug gap too great — spark going to earth (ground).

3. Faulty insulation on sparking plugs.

4. Moisture or dirt in distributor. (NOTE: in desert areas, sand in the distributor is an extremely common fault).

5. Poor battery connections, usually resulting from corrosion between post and cable lug.

6. Short-circuiting from poor wiring insulation.

7. Sticking valve — try a few drops of oil or upper cylinder lubricant in carburettor air intake.

Engine misfires on hard acceleration, but idles well :

8. High-speed jet blocked.

Engine falters at high speed at desert working temperature:

9. Vapour Lock in the Fuel lines — probably near the mani-

fold. Pour water over the line to cool; pull the choke out slightly — the richer mixture will help, and it also has a slightly cooling effect — but remember you are then using more fuel.

Engine shows loss of power on hard acceleration

10. Timing incorrect.

Engine Overheats

1. Fan Belt loose or broken. (Tighten or replace).

2. Timing incorrect — too fast or too slow.

3. Faulty thermostat.

4. Lack of water.

5. Faulty water-pump.

6. Leaking or broken radiator hose.

7. Leaking radiator.

Starter Motor Fails

1. Battery charge low.

2. Starter pinion jammed. (Free by switching off ignition, putting in reverse gear, letting off the handbrake, and rocking the vehicle backwards and forwards).

You can now refer to the Workshop Manual which you undoubtedly have with you!

A Final Word

If you are stuck and in trouble in the desert, don't be afraid to let your imagination work; there is often a tendency to think along lines that are too orthodox when it comes to dealing with mechanical faults. For example, before now vehicles have managed to get to civilisation with a flat tyre, damaged beyond any hope of repair, by stuffing it full of rags, waste material and leaves from shrubs — incredible, but true! On one occasion when my own fuel line broke, I managed to get into a camp by joining the broken ends with plastic tubing from a transfusion set I had with me. Don't forget that there is much material in the bodywork of a vehicle which is non-essential and which you may be able to use **if you think of it** — nuts and bolts from the roof and cab, any number of assorted sizes of screws, insulated wiring to the interior lighting — the list of usable material is large, and often all that is necessary to get the vehicle moving again is to think of a suitable alternative to use for the damaged part.

Summary of Rules for Desert Driving

Before setting out
Check the vehicle
Check your Supplies and Equipment
Make sure you have enough Drinking Water
Record the odometer reading
'Check out'
(Note: it is well worth while making up your own check-list and ticking off each item — this will save you time and make sure you don't forget anything.)

En Route
Never drive in a sandstorm
Never drive at night
If in doubt stop and think
If lost, stop at once
Never leave the vehicle unless you know **exactly** where you are
Stay in the shade as much as possible
Keep a thin layer of clothing on
Avoid strenuous exertion in the middle of the day
'Check in' on arrival

Never Panic.

4. The Camp

A. Site Choice

The desert is unique in that while driving across it you can decide you've had enough for that day, stop, look around and say "Here's where we'll camp tonight". No hunting for suitable sites in a friendly farmer's bull-free field. No searching for a council-permitted caravan park. You just stop, almost anywhere. Almost. But one or two facts should be borne in mind when selecting the site:

1. **Oasis.** If you are near an Oasis, well and good; but beware of the water.

Many oases are inhabited and have open 'wells', and you may even be told that the water has been 'certified pure', as I was on one occasion even while I was actually watching an Arab boy urinating gracefully into the well, in the style of the Brussels mannikin, while a camel, not so gracefully, was defaecating, as had all his immediate and distant family, right on the edge of the water which, in any case, was green with contamination.

'Certified pure' very often means that it has been certified **chemically** pure, which is not at all the same thing as **bacteriologically** pure; surface contamination may be very heavy, and it is no good thinking that because the local inhabitants drink it and look healthy it is O.K; they have been exposed to whatever contamination is present for a long time and undoubtedly have built up a marked resistance to it; but you have not, and are vulnerable.

Sometimes the surface contamination can become so massive that it overcomes even the local resistance. In the well I described above, I was not really surprised 3 weeks later to learn that the whole village had been struck by an outbreak of typhoid! Therefore, you **must** boil **all** water taken from oasis wells before use; but refer to the section on water (pp 64-65). Remember to use some of the boiling water to 'scald' the container in which you collected it in the first place because if the water was infected, then so was the container.

2. **Terrain.** A sandy area is preferable to a rocky one; you will have a much greater freedom from scorpions and probably also snakes; sand is more comfortable if you decide to sleep out; and you are in a much more visible situation if by chance you cannot get the vehicle started in the morning.

3. **Dunes.** If you are camping in an area of dunes, don't fall into the trap of thinking that there will be more shelter at the bottom of the steep side (A); if the wind rises, there will be precious little! This is because the prevailing winds come over the gentle slope, with turbulence resulting where the slope drops away sharply.

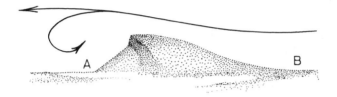

No. Far and away the better position is to the windward (B) exposed and open though it is. The wind may blow strongly there, but at least it will be consistent and not the whirling, omni-directional gusts of the leeward side.

4. **Wadis.** Sometimes, specially near the edges of deserts or near mountains, long gullies can be found, several metres across and of varying depth. Be *Very Careful* about camping in these as they may well be dried out water-courses or Wadis (pronounced 'waddies'), and although they are dried and dead, they are in fact river beds which in the rainy season become highly active.

When the rains descend on the often far distant hills, the water deposited roars down the dried out wadi as a raging brown torrent, possibly as much as 5 metres high, carrying with it bushes, dead sheep, cattle, and on occasions, even men. There is little warning, other than audible, unless you happen to be close enough to the hills to see the storm.

Usually the torrent does not last too long, but its initial eruption can be fierce enough to terrify those who see it. So, in autumn and winter months, camp on the edge of a wadi and you may see an awesome sight, but camp in the wadi and you may well be providing the awesome sight for others!

5.   You can avoid much hostility and trouble by not camping on or near ground which is held to be sacred by the local inhabitants; e.g. tombs, burial grounds or even natural phenomena such as oddly-shaped rocks or, indeed, any feature which immediately strikes the eye by virtue of some obvious peculiarity. An example of the latter is Ayers Rock, in the middle of the Australian outback, which is sacred to the aborigines. You will have to have done your homework before setting out on your trip to know about such areas, but enquiries from your own embassy should suffice. Regarding tombs and burial grounds, remember that with primitive peoples these are likely to be primitive affairs, so it is wise to be wary of any obviously man-made structures — even as simple as piles of stones arranged in a regular fashion; these may well be grave-markers in a cemetery.

B. Layout

The layout, setting-up and hygienic principles of a large desert camp (i.e. for several hundred men) embody all the fundamental principles to be taken into account when dealing with camps for much smaller groups, therefore I shall deal primarily with large ones, referring to any differences as and when they arise.

In considering the layout, three factors must be borne in mind: prevailing wind, slope of the ground, and generator noise. The layout should be such that the prevailing wind will carry all smells of garbage and sewage away from the camp. The Romans used the same principle in always building their colossea and arenas on the lee-side of their cities.

The slope of the ground should be such that the drainage should be naturally away from the camp, that is to say the camp should be on the higher ground.

The generator should also be on the lee-side of the camp; continual generator noise becomes very tiring — witness, for example, the relief you feel when a vacuum cleaner is finally switched off. The same applies with a generator, only more so as it will be running all the time in a large camp. It must be situated well away from the radio and medical units — it is extremely difficult to listen to either a radio message or a heart over the noise of a generator!

For economy of plumbing materials, all buildings or trailers using water should, as far as possible, be arranged in sequence (i.e. kitchens, toilets, showers, medical unit). An example of a typical large desert camp layout embodying these points is as shown on page 58.

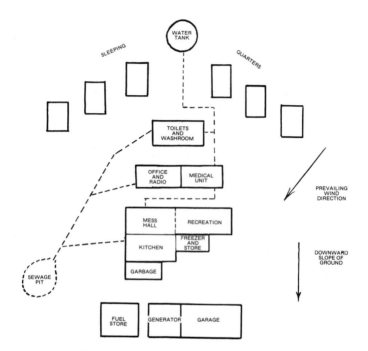

Suggested layout for a large desert camp.

C. Hygiene

This is important anywhere. It is vital in such temperatures as you will encounter, in which food deteriorates and becomes contaminated very rapidly.

1. **Flies** must be controlled from the outset, otherwise life soon becomes very unpleasant, not to mention dangerous. Basic fly control consists of four main procedures:

> Inhibiting breeding, by the prevention or elimination of likely breeding grounds, such as open rubbish dumps, cess-pits, garbage cans or collections of still water (open or leaking drains, etc.).

> Preventing access, by means of fly-screening and well-fitting doors and windows in the larger permanent or semi-permanent camps. In tented camps, however, this is obviously more difficult and therefore destruction of flies is even more important.

> Keeping food covered at all times (*Always* pour opened cans of milk, cream, juices, etc. into jugs which can be covered. If you leave a can opened for even a few minutes, there will be a fly in it, unseen and unsuspected).

> Destroying the adult flies. (see pp 68-69).

2. **Garbage.** Although the desert is vast and empty, under no circumstances must the temptation to scatter garbage indiscriminately be indulged; remember that flies can travel a distance of nearly two kilometres, and they will soon make the trip from a garbage dump to a camp if it is within this distance. Therefore, regardless of the size of your camp, garbage must be transported well away from it to a suitable dump, at least every second day, but preferably daily.

At all times while awaiting transport it must be kept in garbage cans with well-fitting lids, or in the case of smaller camps, in sealed plastic bags. Emptying should be into a previously dug pit, and the garbage then covered with a layer of sand 20-30 cms thick. If particularly offensive or if predominantly wet, it should be first soaked with petrol and burned before covering. Garbage cans should be washed out thoroughly each time they have been emptied, preferably with carbolic or some other strong disinfectant.

A well constructed garbage hut.

In a large camp, if garbage cans cannot be removed and emptied daily, then a fly-proof garbage hut should be constructed so that they may be stored there until such time as they **can** be removed. A loading ramp makes the loading of cans onto a truck much easier (above). Garbage huts should be well ventilated and fly-proofed; they must be kept scrupulously clean by hosing down, insecticides must be used liberally, and the doors should be sprung to make sure they remain closed. They should also be inspected daily as there is a great tendency for them to become dirty as a result of neglect.

3. **Sewage.** Ideally, sewage should run into a pit, downhill from the camp and at least 100 metres from the nearest building or water supply. If at all possible, the sewage pit should be covered, for example with overlapping sheets of corrugated iron or plastic. In sandy areas, however, this is impractical as it is impossible to dig a pit with vertical sides, rather a shallow trench is the result. One can go to the expense of building proper septic tanks of concrete, but an alternative method which I have seen to work exceedingly well was by using empty oil drums. (In large camps there is usually an embarrassingly large number of these, and disposal can be quite a problem.)

In this system, the oil drums have holes punched through their bottom plates and the drums are then joined in series by 10cm pipes high up on the sides, as many drums as it is considered will be needed, and put in a trench which can then be covered with sand. The solids will gradually fill the first drum and then automatically move on to the next, while the liquids soak away through the bottom of the drum. If necessary, more drums can be added if the life of the camp is extended or if they fill up more rapidly than was anticipated.

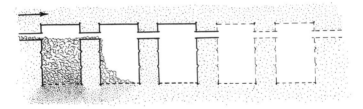

This method has the great advantages that it is safe from fly nuisance and that when the camp finally moves, apart from covering it with sand, nothing further need be done to clean it up.

In small camps, however, such methods are not feasible. In these cases the sewage pit will most probably be open, and if this is so, the resulting pool should be inspected every 2-3 days, layered with oil and burned off.

4. Other Facilities

With regard to the rest of the camp, as I have already said, facilities to be provided are obviously in direct proportion to the size of the camp and the estimated duration of its life. Here are some brief guidance notes:

Kitchens should be kept cool and spotlessly clean; ideally they should be air-conditioned, otherwise doors and windows will be left open to provide air currents, and this of course will allow flies in. In the absence of air-conditioning, an extractor fan is essential. There should be adequate facilities for hand washing — disposable paper towels where possible — but under no circumstances should dishes and cutlery be dried with a towel.

Separate preparation surfaces must be provided for raw meat because of the ease with which contamination can pass from it to other food — e.g. salads, cooked meat, bread. Kitchens should always be thoroughly scrubbed and cleaned after the preparation and serving of any meals. Plenty of refrigeration and deep-freeze space is essential, and care must be taken that they are regularly de-frosted. In small one- or two-man camps, remember that you can 'wash' dishes efficiently by simply scrubbing them with sand, which of course helps to conserve your water supplies.

Toilets, whether flushing, chemical or of a more primitive type, must be kept fly-proof, clean and disinfected. If they are not, this encourages indiscriminate urinating and defaecating in the neighbourhood of the camp which at one stroke will counter-act all efforts at hygiene elsewhere.

Washrooms and Showers, like everything else, must be kept clean; leaks must be repaired as soon as they occur, obviously to stop wastage, but also to prevent pools of water collecting and forming a breeding ground for our old friends the flies. Showers are not a luxury only for large camps. There is a type of shower available for you even if you are travelling alone, and one which is very economical of water. It consists of a rubber foot-pump attached to about 2 metres length of tubing, ending in a circle of perforated tubing. All you need to do is stand in a basin of water with the ring around your neck and pump with your foot. Admittedly you will be using the same water over and over again, but if you want you can make a shower last two hours with the expenditure of only a couple of litres of water!

Sleeping accommodation should of course be kept clear of sand. Sand gets into everything, and you would very soon find that it might be more pleasant sleeping on an open desert of sand than with even just a handful of it in your bed! Blankets should have the sand beaten out of them at least weekly, and a periodic search for bed-bugs, lice and vermin carried out.

In small overnight camps, it is specially important to remember that overnight temperatures fall very dramatically - it is by no means unusual in the winter to find temperatures of 70°F in the afternoon yielding to below freezing the following morning, so if you are not prepared for this you are going to be in for pretty miserable nights.

If you are camping in a tent, it is wise to get one with a 'mud-cloth' round the bottom - i.e. an extra flap which lies on the ground when the tent is erected; by covering this flap with sand it effectively seals off the tent from sand blowing in around the sides. Even better, of course, is one with an integral, stitched-in ground sheet 'floor'.

Tent pegs are useless in soft sand, and the best way of securing a tent is by using the Bedouin method of tying each guy-rope to a small scrub bush and burying it. Such bushes, of course, are found only in scrub desert, so if you are going deeper into the desert, make sure you don't discard them once used; also, if you cut them, rather than dig them up, you will leave the roots in to grow again.

Most tent fabrics are treated with a flame-resistant material but this does **not** mean that they will not catch fire if you are cooking inside them, or if the wind changes and blows sparks from an outside fire on to the tent, so do bear this in mind.

Should you be travelling in a small group, or even alone, and have no tent or sleeping bag, you may very well find that rather than sleep in your vehicle you will be more comfortable if you dig a 'bed' in the sand and cover it with your plastic sheeting; as long as there is not too much space left for the air to get in, you should be reasonably warm and very comfortable.

Finally, when you are moving on, **please** leave the camp site as it was when you found it, not least of all for your own sake; it is amazing what articles, valuable or otherwise, are often left behind and which would have been found had a final clear-up been done. It really doesn't take long to dig a hole and shove your rubbish in, then cover it up, along with the garbage and sewage pits. This may seem trivial — after all, the desert is enormous — but the exciting reality of being alone in a vast empty desert is abruptly ruined when you come across the untidy remnants of someone else's camp!

D. Water Supplies

With the absence of rain and lakes, water in the desert is generally obtained from wells or else is imported from the nearest towns or oases. In a surprisingly large number of areas there is water in the desert only 1½-2 metres below the surface; such water however, is usually unpalatable and in any case should be bacteriologically and chemically tested for potability before being used as drinking water; and, even if found to be suitable for drinking, the source of supply must be at least 70 metres away from cess-pits or sewage lines.

The deeper the water-level is found below the surface, however, the more likely it is to be free from surface contamination and therefore the more likely it is to be safe to drink.

Water Testing for potability is a highly specialised business which must be left to the resources of a skilled laboratory; the most widely used tests are those in which the technician searches for evidence of faecal contamination in the form of coliform organisms found only in the intestinal tract of man and animals.

Local knowledge of the sources of supply in any given area is as essential as bacteriological testing - i.e. water may be found to have a low enough 'coliform count' one day to be able to certify it as potable, but this is of no value unless you also know that the source is free from danger of surface pollution. It follows therefore that water taken from any natural sources in the desert **must** be purified before using it for drinking, in the preparation of food or even for cleaning your teeth!

Water Purification can be carried out in a number of ways and it is not intended to cover them all here. However, a few of the simpler methods should be mentioned.

1. **Boiling:** Boiling is a useful and universally known method of sterilising water in emergencies, and will kill nearly all of the common bacteria causing ill-health. It will not kill sporing bacteria. If the un-boiled water is not clear, it is advisable to strain it through fine cloth, prior to boiling for 5 minutes.

2. **Bleaching Powder:** This makes an effective water-sterilising agent in the proper dilution: dissolve 5 ml (1 teaspoonful) in 1 litre of water. Add 5 ml of this mixture to every 10 litres of water to be sterilised, and leave for 20-30 minutes before using.

3. **Halazone Tablets:** These useful tablets are made up in inexpensive bottles of 1,000, and can be purchased at most pharmacies and chemists. They are effective against most of the commoner forms of contamination. 1 or 2 tablets — according to the degree of contamination — should be added to each litre of water which is then shaken; after the tablets have dissolved the water should not be used for half an hour.

4. **Filters:** There are many water filters on the market today so I will only mention two of them, which I have found to be reliable.

Katadyn filters operate by means of ceramic 'candles' which have extremely fine pores, are impregnated with silver and have an inner filling of silver quartz; the silver renders them self-disinfecting. The passage of water through these candles from the outside filters off bacteria and suspended matter which collect on the surface of the candles; this means that the candles have to be brushed clean periodically, and at the same time they must be inspected for cracks. A cracked candle is useless and must be discarded at once, and if you find that the rate of flow of filtered water increases, then the candles must once again be inspected immediately for cracks. These filters come in a variety of sizes and are suitable for very large camps as permanent fixtures plumbed in to the water supply, or for the solo traveller as portable, individual appliances. (see Appendix B). Used sensibly they fulfill their function admirably.

Safari filters work on much the same principle, but use patented cartridges rather than candles. Special features are that the cartridge is flexible and so does not need to be inspected for cracks, that it is heat-resistant and can be used with hot water, and that when the time comes to replace the cartridge, this will be self-evident as the flow will cease - i.e. when the flow of purified water becomes too slow, you must replace the cartridge. These filters, like the Katadyn, are efficient and effective and can be obtained in a variety of sizes (see Appendix B).

E. Personal Hygiene

Clothing: Above all, clothes must be comfortable, and should therefore be:

1. Light in Weight
2. Light in Colour
3. Loose fitting
4. Washable

You cannot go far wrong if you stick to these four requirements, apart from those who need special clothing for their particular work - for example, welders. Avoid Nylon at all costs in climates where you will be sweating; you will keep cooler wearing clothes than if you take them off (see page 43).

Cotton underclothing is by far the best and should be changed daily; with the inevitable increased amount of sweating, frequent washing of all clothes - and underclothes in particular - is essential. Remember to allow for this in estimating your water requirements. If you follow this recommendation, you will need the minimum of clothing, and space is valuable. Certain drip-dry polyester clothing — e.g. Dacron — is suitable for desert conditions if you do not have pure cotton.

Footwear: While open sandals undoubtedly are the most hygienic form of footwear, unfortunately they are not the most practical as they offer no protection from snakes, scorpions or toe injuries; probably the most efficient form of footgear is an above-the-ankle light-weight boot; shoes are not to be recommended if the terrain consists mainly of soft sand as there is no support given to the ankle, and sand continually manages to get inside the shoe which soon becomes uncomfortable.

On a personal note, in sandy desert conditions I always used to wear open, thonged sandals which I found to be very comfortable as obviously the sand could not remain in them. One day, however, I witnessed something which changed my thinking instantly. What I saw was a viper, in open desert, disappear in front of my very eyes! A few side-to-side wriggles and he had gone, sinking beneath the sand with the sole exception of one eye which remained fixed intently on me yet looking exactly like a tiny black pebble. Until then I would never have believed that a snake could have disappeared so utterly and completely, leaving no trace of any sort, and yet still be there watching me! From then on, it was desert boots for me!

Gloves: Don't forget to take an old pair of tough gloves with you - very useful for the really mucky jobs on the vehicle, and they save you having to waste water scrubbing your hands afterwards.

Skin cleanliness: You should shower, or wash completely, at least once daily when the weather is hot, for two reasons:

1. It is comfortable and refreshing.

2. Moist, sweaty skin is an ideal breeding ground for bacteria and fungi.

Drying must be scrupulously carried out, with particular attention to the skin crevices, toes, groin, armpits and the rectal area. Any traces of fungal infection in the groin or between the toes should be treated as soon as you notice them - see 'Common Ailments'.

F. Flies and Other Insects

House Flies: The common House Fly is to be found all over the world, but nowhere does it seem to be quite so arrogant and annoying as in the desert. It is a revolting unhygenic insect with revolting unhygenic habits, and is probably one of the biggest single factors in the transmission of diseases. It should be looked on as a real threat, and not just a nuisance.

House Fly Enlarged   Life Size (8mm)

Here are a few facts about flies which you may not know:

They generally have a bowel action while eating.

They eat by vomiting onto their food, then sucking back their vomit.

They constantly alight on faecal matter, decayed and rotting meat, garbage and filth of any kind, and then quite possibly on YOUR food.

The female fly lays about 120 eggs at a time, and **in only 8 weeks a single female fly will have given rise to half a million descendants! It is obviously easier, therefore, to kill one fly today than to have to rush around in 8 weeks time trying to kill 500,000!**

Because of their filthy habits, they transmit germs on their hairy bodies, legs and foot-pads; they can AND DO transmit bacteria and other infective agents which cause the following diseases:-
Typhoid, Paratyphoid, Dysentery, Cholera, Anthrax, Trachoma, Tropical Sores, Worms. Flight range is up to 2 kilometres.

It follows that you cannot begin to eliminate this threat too early; control over the fly menace is gained by (1) efficient disposal of sewage and garbage (see 'Camp Hygiene'), and (2) destruction of the flies themselves by swatters, Vapona sticks, insecticides (see appendix) or even the old-fashioned fly-papers which are free from the risk of chemical contamination of food in kitchens, and which are at least as efficient.

Mosquitoes: The two main groups of mosquitoes are (1) Anopheles, the female of which is the vector (carrier) of Malaria, and (2) Culex, one variety of which is the vector of Yellow Fever. (There are over 300 varieties of Anopheles and over 2,000 varieties of Culex mosquitoes).

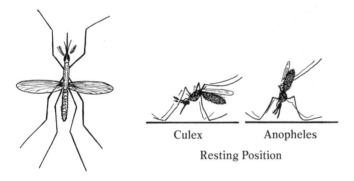

Culex   Anopheles

Resting Position

Mosquitoes breed in shallow pools of stagnant water and take 8 days to reach full maturity from the egg, though they may take longer in cooler climates. Anopheles are generally night-biters, but some forms of Culex have a tendency to bite by day. Flight range of mosquitoes is 1-2 kilometres. Control is by the elimination of any likely breeding grounds and destruction of the adults. Distinction between Anopheles and Culex groups is easy if you can see the mosquito at rest - the Anopheles' body is in a straight line angled to the surface on which it is resting, the Culex's body is humped.

Fleas: There are over 1,500 different species of fleas, all of which are blood-suckers; they are very hard, flat (side-ways) and small, about 2-3 mm. During development the pupal stage of the flea may remain dormant for as long as 2 years. Generally they cause only irritating bites, but they can also transmit Plague (the rat flea), Typhus and the eggs of some tapeworms.

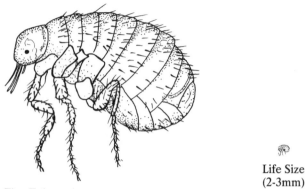

Life Size
(2-3mm)

Flea Enlarged

The **Sandflea** ('Chigger Flea') used to be found only in the West Indies and Tropical America, but is now found in East Africa. It is like the common flea in appearance, but the females produce their eggs beneath the skin of warm-blooded animals including man, burrowing under the skin of the feet or fingers, giving rise to very troublesome ulcers, through which there is a risk of contracting Tetanus.

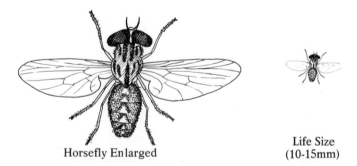

Horsefly Enlarged

Life Size
(10-15mm)

Horseflies are large insects and strong fliers; they give a painful bite and may transmit infection from other sources in their bite. They breed in swampy, sluggish water and streams, and so are to be found mainly in coastal edges of deserts.

Midges (often known as Biting Midges) are found all over the world and are of no real medical importance apart from their nuisance value; they are dawn and dusk biters, and have a flight range of 150-350 metres, depending on the wind.

Sandfly Enlarged   Life Size (1 - 3mm)

Sandflies are very small and hairy, and are to be found in drier parts of the Tropics and Subtropics; their flight range is not more than 50 metres. They are transmitters of Sandfly Fever.

Simulium Fly Enlarged   Life Size

Simulium Flies ('Buffalo Flies') are small, only 2-4mm in length, and are to be found all over the world. They have a flight range of up to 30 kms from their breeding places, their larvae always being found in flowing water. They are important as the transmitters of Onchocerciasis, which is a filarial worm infestation of man.

Tse Tse Fly Enlarged

Life Size

Tsetse Flies are large, about 6-14 mm in length, with stiff, prominent probosces. They are confined to tropical Africa, for the most part living in forest and savannah regions. Medically, they are extremely important as the transmitters of Sleeping Sickness (Trypanosomiasis).

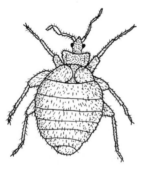

Life Size

Bedbug Enlarged

Bed Bugs are flat, round and small, about 5 mm in length. They do not transmit disease but give irritating bites. They mainly infest crevices and cracks in woodwork — floors, behind wooden walls, etc.

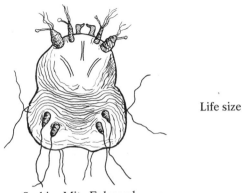

Life size

Scabies Mite Enlarged

The Scabies Mite is distributed all over the world, but specially in North Africa; it burrows beneath human skin where the female lays her eggs, commonly in legs, thighs and skin folds and creases. Infestation with Scabies usually indicates dirty clothing and unhygienic habits.

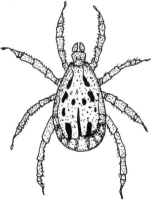

Life Size

Hard Tick Enlarged

Ticks are of world-wide distribution and are very important as transmitters of disease. They are classified into 'Hard' and 'Soft' varieties. Soft Ticks are common in Central Africa and live in thatch, and in cracks in walls, floors and roofs; they transmit Relapsing Fever and some virus diseases. Hard Ticks develop through many stages in different hosts and transmit Typhus, virus diseases and bacteriological diseases.

Cockroaches are also to be found anywhere in the world and are one of the oldest insects known to man. They will eat anything but must have a source of water nearby. Infestation with cockroaches generally indicates lack of cleanliness and the presence of food particles. Apart from the mechanical transmission of bacteria by their bodies to food, their medical importance is limited.

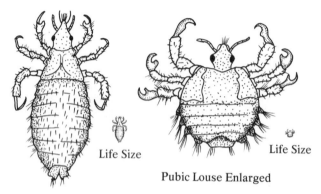

Life Size

Life Size

Pubic Louse Enlarged

Body Louse Enlarged

Lice are flat, whitish insects of which there are three main types:

1. Body Louse (Pediculus Corporis)
2. Head Louse (Pediculus Capitis)
3. Pubic Louse (Pediculus Pubis - 'Crab')

The body louse and head louse are very active and can move surprisingly rapidly, specially when they are warm, — e.g. if the infested person has a fever. Lice generally inhabit the seams of clothing in which the eggs are laid; the eggs (nits) of the head louse are actually stuck to the hairs with a type of cement, and must be carefully removed at the same time as the lice are being treated. Lice can transmit Relapsing Fever and Typhus.

5. Heat and Health

Common Sense and Health

It is important to keep a sense of reality about health in the desert. As a result of excessive heat, vast distances and a feeling of being 'cut off' from civilisation, trivial ailments often become magnified in the mind into dreadful signs of some impending health disaster; if one has a fertile imagination — as do many of those who are attracted to the desert — there is a real danger of worrying unduly when the odd pain or ache occurs, but it is quite extraordinary how rapidly most of these will disappear when one is back in civilisation again!

Heat and the Body

When people move to a hot climate their bodies have to undergo a period of acclimatisation; when they first move into these regions it is found that:

1. Physical effort cannot be prolonged, and exhaustion occurs easily.

2. The pulse rate rises - i.e. the heart beats at a faster rate.

3. The body temperature tends to rise.

In other words, in the very early days in a hot climate you will be apt to feel hot and exhausted after a very little effort. After about 8-10 days, however, you will find that:

1. Physical effort can be maintained for much longer periods without exhaustion.

2. The pulse rate rises much more slowly and not to the same extent as previously.

3. The body temperature is much more stable.

This is to say, you have become 'Acclimatised'.

The reason for this lies simply in sweating. The more you sweat, the more body heat you lose; therefore in a hot climate the more you can sweat — within reason — the more efficient is the maintenance of your body temperaturee at an ideal level.

The sweat glands of the skin, however, like the muscles of an athlete, have to be trained to work harder when extra demand is placed on them, and this takes time; so, until they are trained, sweat loss is not generally sufficient to enable the body temperature to remain at a good working level, and exhaustion results. An unacclimatised man will secrete only half the volume of sweat that 8-10 days later he will be secreting when he is acclimatised.

Basically, all this means is that during the first two weeks you must not expect to be capable of your full, normal range of activity.

Note: It is of a slight advantage to be lean rather than too fat, because a lean person has a **relatively** larger skin area per kilo of body weight and therefore can sweat more for his weight than a fat person; thus thin people can usually acclimatise more rapidly than fat people. (You may have noticed that, generally speaking, heavier people are to be found in the cooler climates, and thinner people in the hotter climates.)

The Question of Salt and Water

This is important, and well worth a few minutes' effort to understand.

If sweat has ever trickled down your face and into your mouth you will realise from the taste that it contains a lot of salt, and salt is vital for the proper functioning of the body. Because it is important to sweat in the tropics, it is **equally important** to replace both the salt and water which are continually being lost in the sweat; obviously it follows that you will require a lot more salt and water in a hot climate than a temperate one.

Salt Deficiency: In desert climates, salt deficiency is a condition which generally arises slowly, and usually in people who have access to abundant water; i.e. they sweat, losing salt and water, become thirsty and so drink water without thinking about the salt. In this way, the salt content of their bodies gradually becomes more and more depleted until the symptoms of salt deficiency become noticeable; these symptoms are weariness, lassitude and often muscular cramps, and are very rapidly eased by the taking of salt. You will find it quite extraordinary how much salt you can tolerate **and enjoy** when you are suffering from a deficiency. Salt can be taken in food, in water, or as tablets; the most satisfactory method of taking extra salt is by adding it to drinking water — approximately 1 gram per litre.

Water Deficiency: This condition can arise rapidly, *and will be made worse if you eat salt,* as the more salt you take, the more water you must take to keep the salt in solution. The average man doing physical work in desert conditions needs to drink 10 litres (17 pints) **minimum** each day — any less will sooner or later lead to symptoms of deficiency.

Both Salt deficiency and Water deficiency will reduce a man's working and thinking capabilities and, if extreme, can be very serious indeed.

Water deficiency can also arise slowly as a chronic, unnoticed condition; for example, one of the ailments which occurs more frequently in the desert than I should have originally thought is renal colic — caused by 'stones' (small concretions of crystallised salts) becoming jammed in the urinary tract and causing acute spasmodic pain. The cause of this is not difficult to find — chronic water insufficiency, which leads to urine becoming concentrated to such an extent that salts (e.g. phosphates and urates) which are normally held in solution tend to crystallise out to form stones.

The odd thing, however, was that these attacks of renal colic were occuring in men living in and working from very well organised camps, with showers, ice-machines and virtually limitless water, so it was difficult to understand why this should be a problem.

The answer, of course, lay in the fact that the common practice was to drink enough to satisfy the thirst; this, per se, is not enough to re-hydrate the body, and over a period of some weeks the body will become progressively more dehydrated. Virtually without exception the affected men, when asked about their frequency of passing urine, would firstly be puzzled and say they hadn't thought about it and then say something like "twice a day" (never more) — in fact one memorable chap said he couldn't remember when he had last passed urine!

The rule, therefore, is to **drink sufficient to keep you passing urine as frequently as is your normal practice** and not just enough to satisfy your thirst; the urine should be pale and straw-coloured — if very dark it is too concentrated.

To recapitulate: if you are in a hot climate, sweating freely and have plenty of water to drink, then make sure you are having enough extra salt; if, however, in the same climate you are stuck with a severely limited water supply, do NOT take salt. (I should like to suggest that you read this whole section, 'The Question of Salt and Water', again — it is VERY important.)

Heat Illnesses

We have seen the mechanism by which body temperature is maintained at a constant level in a hot climate; if this level is not maintained then some form of heat illness — or more correctly, 'heat disorder' — will result. The most important forms of heat disorder are as follows:

1. Heat Syncope

2. Heat Exhaustion: a. Water deficiency

b. Salt deficiency

3. Heat Hyperpyrexia

Heat Syncope. This is really a simple 'faint' though it can be alarming to onlookers who see it for the first time. It is due to the sudden dilatation of the surface blood vessels as a result of standing for a long period or hard physical effort in heat; because of this dilatation, the blood pressure drops, and the patient becomes white and falls down in a faint. Recovery occurs rapidly and spontaneously and can be accelerated by forcing the patient's head down between his knees. The condition is not serious.

Heat Exhaustion. The two forms of this have already been considered under 'The Question of Salt and Water', and there is little more to be added beyond the fact that recovery is generally rapid — except in very severe cases — when the appropriate deficiency is remedied.

Heat Hyperpyrexia. This is a serious condition, but not one that is very common; it generally affects people who are not yet acclimatised, specially the young or elderly.

Diagnosis depends on the presence of three signs:

1. Unconsciousness (usually sudden)

2. High Fever

3. Absence of Sweating.

The shorter the period of unconsciousness, the better the outlook. Treatment consists mainly in reducing the fever, and this can be done by bathing in cold or iced water, using a fan if available or even wrapping the patient in a wet sheet. However, skilled medical aid should be sought at the earliest opportunity, as there are other serious medical conditions which present themselves in a similar manner.

Sunburn

Sunburn results from excessive exposure of the skin to the ultra-violet rays of the sun, and may vary from a tingling redness to painful blistering; it usually tends to be more severe in fair- and red-headed people than in the dark-haired.

Prevention is always better than cure, by taking care not to expose the unaccustomed skin to the sun for too long too early, and in this respect sun-filter creams are very useful — e.g. 'Club Mediterrané' (L'Oreal), Uvistat, Ambre Solaire, Bergasol; the higher the filter number of the preparation, the greater the protection. When it comes to treatment, there are many excellent preparations on the market, but a simple and effective home remedy is to use as a lotion a mixture of equal parts of vinegar and water. Antihistamines such as Benadryl, or Caladryl Lotion, will also help, but remember that sunburn is like any other burn, and the tissues are damaged; therefore it will take its own time to heal, regardless of what you do for it.

Blisters should **not** be burst — try to preserve them intact with plenty of talcum powder and a soft pad of cotton wool; once they do burst, then the way is clear for infection to enter. Blistering and swelling under the eyes must be left alone — if **very** severe, seek medical aid if available.

Don't be too concerned if, the day following burning (specially on the forehead), you have difficulty in getting your eyes open due to swelling; a lot of this is caused by laying flat during the night, and it will almost certainly improve after you have been up for a short time.

Prickly Heat

This is an annoying affliction to those who suffer from it; it generally occurs in those parts of the body where air-flow over the surface is restricted — armpits, waist, groin, etc.—or where clothing is too tight. Although in itself not serious, prickly heat can be extremely distressing by interfering with sleep and if this continues then it does become serious. So, keep clothing loose, light and to a minimum, and avoid nylon; frequent washing, very careful drying and the use of a talcum powder, or 'Prickly Heat Powder', will do much to prevent its occurence.

6 Ailments: Serious And Not So!

Note: This section is not intended to take the place of orthodox medical treatment or to create a group of 'do-it-yourself' amateur doctors! It is purely intended to help the traveller who is far from medical aid and who is not quite sure what to do if he has the misfortune to be afflicted by sickness, and also to put some of the ailments into a wider and more general perspective.

Athlete's Foot:

Fungus infections such as Athlete's Foot have a great tendency to flare up in hot and humid climates, therefore scrupulous cleanliness is essential. Treat by:-

Frequent washing of the feet (at least twice daily) and thorough drying.

Twice daily applications of anti-fungal powder such as Asterol or Tineafax to the lesions between the toes, to the socks and inside the shoes, after washing the feet.

Daily change of socks; socks should be boiled, which of course means that they should be cotton.

Backstrain:

This usually results from lifting a heavy object in the wrong manner, using the back muscles rather than the leg ones. Treat by rest on a **firm** support — put the mattress on the floor if necessary — and give pain-relieving tablets such as Aspirin or Paracetamol. Avoid exertion till the pain has completely settled. If the backache is accompanied by tingling down one — or both — legs, then a medical checkup is indicated when convenient.

Bilharzia: See page 85.

Bleeding Nose:

This is hardly ever as serious as it seems! Most bleeding noses result from the rupture of a small artery in the front of the nose on the septum between the nostrils, and can be controlled quite simply by pinching the end of the nose firmly between the fingers. BUT, keep pinching for 10 minutes, resisting the temptation to let go to see if it has stopped before the 10 minutes are up; do NOT blow your nose to clear the clot out after it has stopped — the clot is what has stopped it and there is no surer way of starting it off again than by blowing the clot out; do not blow it for 24 hours, and even then only very gently. Do NOT stoop — e.g. to wash your face or to tie up your shoe-laces — stooping raises local blood pressure in your head and nose and this may blow the clot out and start it bleeding again. Lastly, do NOT lie down while the nose is bleeding, for the same reason; sit straight up and breathe quietly through your mouth.

Cuts and Abrasions:

Clean gently with gauze swab and peroxide. Apply Merthiolate or, if there is much rawness, Terramycin or Penicillin ointment. Cover with gauze swab and bandage.

If the cut is gaping, clean as above, use Terramycin ointment, and draw edges together with adhesive tape or suture strips before bandaging. Do not get the dressing wet, and leave in place for 2-3 days, unless the wound starts to throb and swell, in which case it must be inspected for secondary infection; if it is secondarily infected (red, hot and/or discharging) then the wound must be cleaned thoroughly at least once a day, then re-dressed.

If the cut is spurting blood, then it means that a small artery has been severed; treat with firm pressure pad and bandage (see page 106) but if this does not control the bleeding you may have to apply a tourniquet (see page 111); this is a last resort, however, and should not be used unless you have no alternative, in which case the rules for tourniquets must be STRICTLY observed.

Deafness:

Deafness is not uncommon in the desert due to catarrh in the Eustachian tube behind the eardrum; in most cases, the deafness is of short duration only. Wax in the ear does not appear to be such a problem as might have been expected.

Deafness without discharge or pain: this is most likely due to the catarrhal condition mentioned above, and must be treated **through the nose,** not the ear. Put 4-5 drops of Ephedrine nose drops up each nostril 4-5 times daily and eventually it should clear; if it does not, then the ear should be examined by a doctor.

Deafness with pain, or with discharge: This type of deafness should be examined as soon as possible; if you are a long way from help but do have penicillin tablets with you, then take 1 tablet every four hours (2 for the first dose), and Paracetamol or aspirin for the pain. Have your ears checked when possible.

Diabetic Emergencies

If you are travelling with someone who is a known diabetic, he will certainly know how to deal with his condition himself. However, there is one problem with which he may need help and this is known as **Hypoglycaemia,** almost always occurring in diabetics who are dependent on insulin injections. In hypoglycaemia, the blood sugar falls to a dangerously low level, due to either too large a dose of insulin or too much activity burning up the blood sugar too quickly (such as digging-out a bogged-down vehicle). As a result, the patient becomes rapidly and progressively more confused and irritable. (He will also be sweating, but in the desert heat, so probably will you!)

Untreated, he will rapidly go into a coma, so prompt action is essential. He must take sugar, or preferably glucose, at once; generally he knows this and will do so, but if the blood sugar is low enough his resulting confusion may be sufficient to make him forget this, or even to dispute his need for sugar, so you must force him to eat some — 2-3 lumps, or else water with a similar amount dissolved in it to drink. Recovery will be rapid and complete within 10 minutes after he has taken his sugar.

However, should he already be in a coma (unconscious and impossible to rouse) then you must give him an injection of Glucagon (and an insulin-dependant diabetic travelling away from home should always have this with him). (See appendix, page 125 and 'How to......', page110). As soon as he is recovering consciousness enough to be able to swallow, give him sugar, then a sandwich, cake or sweet biscuit to eat. It is obvious that, before starting out on a trip, the diabetic should make certain, for his own protection, that his fellow travellers know how and when to administer Glucagon — and where he keeps it!

Dysentery and Diarrhoea

The word 'dysentery' to some intending travellers implies a dreaded threat which hangs ominously over anyone who is foolish enough to leave his home country and travel abroad. Certainly, most travellers abroad do suffer, at one time or another, from mild — or not so mild — diarrhoea from which they usually recover rapidly, and which, in some cases, enables them to tell their non-travelling friends, with just a touch of pride, about "my dysentery"! So let us consider exactly what is meant by the term 'dysentery'.

The first thing to realise is that there is no such *disease* as dysentery — the word dysentery refers to various groups of upsets, all with diarrhoea as a common feature.

There are three main groups of dysentery:

1. Dysenteries due to Bacilli ('germs').

2. Dysenteries due to Protozoa.

3. Dysenteries due to Worms.

1. Dysenteries due to Bacilli.

Bacillary Dysentery may range in severity from mild, so-called 'summer diarrhoea' to an illness severe enough to cause death, usually from dehydration. It is frequently liable to occur in epidemics, specially in hot, unhygienic conditions in spring and autumn. Owing to modern methods of treatment bacillary dysentery is no longer the serious threat that it used to be.

Causes of bacillary dysentery are:

a. Contamination of food by flies.

b. Contamination of food and milk by other means.

c. Contamination of water.

d. Lack of Acquired Immunity to the various infecting agents by recent arrivals to a new area.

An attack of bacillary dysentery affects the large intestine causing inflammation and, in long-standing or severe cases, ulcers of the bowel lining. It gives rise to the following group of **symptoms:**

Diarrhoea, mild or acute, with the passage of frequent loose, mucous stools which may or may not contain blood.

Griping abdominal pains, usually central, which vary greatly in severity; generally, the more acute the infection, the more the diarrhoea and the greater the abdominal pain.

Sometimes Fever.

Sometimes Vomiting.

Occasionally Muscular cramps in limb and abdominal muscles due to prolonged fluid loss diminishing the body's supply of salt.

Treatment of Bacillary Dysentery:

Bed

Give plenty of fluids — water, squashes, etc., — to replace what is being lost in the diarrhoea.

Give salt tablets or salt solution if muscular cramps are evident.

Give NO SOLID FOOD for the first 24 hours; then, as the symptoms lessen, gradually increase to a light, easily digestible diet (soups, jellies, etc.). Normal diet should not be resumed until at least 24 hours have passed without diarrhoea. A useful guide is that no foods that need to be chewed should be eaten during this period — too much solid bulk will only tend to re-aggravate the recovering inflamed intestine and start the whole thing off again.

Give Sulphaguanidine, 0.5 gm tablets, in an adult dose of four to begin with, then two every 4 hours, till about 14 have been taken.

Local Warmth (not heat) to abdomen.

Ideally, the patient should be resting in bed for a full day after —

a. Temperature is down to Normal.

b. Abdominal pain has ceased, and

c. Diarrhoea has ceased.

Even then, when he first gets up the patient will be surprisingly weak and convalescence should be gentle if recurrences are to be avoided.

Of course, in severe cases, or cases which do not respond satisfactorily to treatment with Sulphaguanidine, skilled medical aid should be sought.

2. Dysenteries due to Protozoa

Amoebic Dysentery is a disease which is due to infestation with specific protozoa, Entamoeba Histolytica, and which is more common in tropical and subtropical regions than in Europe, though it is not unknown there; it is widespread in the Middle East and Far East and in the Southern U.S.A.

Amoebic dysentery is a disease of insanitation, and outbreaks can occur at any time, though generally cases tend to arise singly rather than in epidemics; however, if one member of a family is infected it is likely that some of the other members also will be. The **sources of infection** include water and fresh vegetables: spread is by flies or rodents. The incubation period (between infection and development of symptoms) is likely to be long, usually several weeks or even months, and the disease runs a long chronic course in which it improves and then flares up again many times.

Symptoms:

> Diarrhoea, usually not too severe, and recurring from time to time; the stools often contain old blood, said to be like 'Anchovy Sauce' in appearance.

> Abdominal tenderness, rather than acute pain.

> Fever may occur, but it is not common.

> Vomiting is rare.

Diagnosis and Treatment of Amoebic dysentery should always be carried out under skilled medical supervision with laboratory stool tests to confirm the diagnosis, then later to check up that the infection is clear, and remains clear; in untreated or incompletely treated cases, the disease may progress to give rise to abscesses in the liver, haemorrhage from the bowel or perforation of the intestine, therefore periodic follow-up stool tests are essential.

3. Dysenteries due to Worms.

Bilharzia (Schistosomiasis). Although not a true dysentery, Bilharzia is a disease of enormous importance and rapidly increasing incidence which sometimes gives rise to 'Schistosomal Dysentery' and therefore it is worth considering briefly here.

It occurs in practically the whole of Africa, Arabia, the Caribbean and the Far East, and it is estimated that it effects 1 in 20 of all human beings. The parasite which causes the disease is a flat, elongated 'Trematode' worm, transmitted by fresh-water snails in which the worm undergoes a development stage in its life cycle to produce a tiny, free-swimming organism; this organism is capable of penetrating intact skin and immediately after it has done this it gives rise to intense irritation — 'Bather's Itch' — which lasts about an hour.

Having thus gained entry to the body of man through the skin, the parasite then travels to the liver and undergoes a further development stage lasting about 6 weeks. At the end of this time, the by now fully developed male and female worms travel via the blood-stream to their ultimate goals, usually the bladder or intestine, according to which species they are; here they lay their eggs which are passed out in the urine or faeces, hatching into another free-swimming form which again will enter the body of a snail, and the whole cycle begins once more. This complete development cycle takes a total of 10-12 weeks, and the adult worms can live for up to 20 years.

The disease has been known for at least 4,000 years — the Egyptians 'invented' circumcision to prevent it, as they thought it gained entry via the penis.

Symptoms of Bilharzia are variable, according to the stage of the disease and which parts of the body are mostly affected, but may comprise:

'Bather's Itch'.

The presence of blood in the urine, generally appearing at the end of the act of micturition.

Enlargement of the liver and spleen, with fever, headaches, aching muscles, and all other accompaniments of fever.

Frequent blood-stained loose motions — the so-called Schistosomal dysentery.

The severity of the disease varies greatly, many of the sufferers experiencing very little discomfort.

Treatment is a matter of skilled medical and surgical investigation to evaluate the type and stage of the disease, followed by the appropriate method of treatment; this should be carried out in hospital, with long-term follow-up after discharge; treatment usually results in a satisfactory cure, if the condition has not lasted too long before diagnosis.

Foreign Material in the Eye:

Few minor conditions are so annoying or painful as this. To inspect an eye for foreign bodies, the best way is to stand **behind** the patient who should be seated with his head back; hold upper and lower eyelids widely separated and then inspect each corner of the eye in turn, getting the patient to move his eye as required to let you inspect the area you wish. A casual glance is not enough — you must really search.

Don't forget to look under the upper lid, and to do this you must get the patient to look downwards, place a match across the root of the eyelid and then, pulling gently on the lashes, fold the lid back upwards till you have completely everted it; now you will be able to see the whole surface of the lid.

Once you see the foreign body, then with a wisp of moistened cotton wool, very gently try to lift it out, holding the lids wide open. In most cases, it will come away quite easily, but if it does not then you must leave it strictly alone; put a pad over the eye, strapping it firmly in place, and get medical aid as soon as possible, as it is most likely that the eye will have to be anaesthetised before the foreign material can be removed.

Once the eye is clear of foreign material, it is wise to put in a few drops of Albucid, or some antibiotic eye ointment.

In a sandstorm it is frequently found that a great deal of sand gets into the eye; this generally washes out easily with Optrex, or even with plain water.

Haemorrhoids:

As a result of heavy sweating, dehydration and resulting constipation, haemorrhoids (piles) are fairly common. These can be pretty uncomfortable, or even very painful indeed; therefore it is worth keeping the bowels free and avoiding constipation, and one of the easiest ways of doing this is just to make sure that you drink plenty of fluid. If you do develop a haemorrhoid, then apply an anti-haemorrhoid ointment such as Anusol or Nupercainal, making certain that the area is kept very clean with frequent washing. If the piles are bleeding, then it may be necessary to wear some sort of a pad, which is often quite a good idea anyway as it does give some support to the piles and eases some of the discomfort.

For an acute attack of piles, it is necessary to rest in bed till they have subsided, then get surgical advice on return to civilization.

Heat Disorders:

See page 78.

Indigestion:

Most sufferers from indigestion have their own favourite remedies which they will defend against all others; most of these remedies, however, rely purely and simply on a large content of Bicarbonate of Soda, or some similar antacid. Indigestion is usually due to an inflamed stomach lining ('gastritis') producing an excess of Hydrochloric acid, the main ingredient of gastric juice. Such inflammation results from many causes, and in such cases, the irritated stomach tends to empty very rapidly; the hydrochloric acid of the gastric juice will then tend to irritate the stomach further.

You can relieve the symptoms by reversing the process:

> Give this extra acid something to work on — i.e. put some sort of food into your stomach every 2-2½ hours — even a glass of milk will work. It is always a good rule to eat **little and often,** rather than to have large, widely separated meals.
>
> Neutralise the excess acid — this is where the favourite antacid remedies come in useful.
>
> Avoid the types of food that are irritating to the stomach, such as fats, spices, alcohol, and fruits rich in acid.
>
> Try to rest for half an hour or so after each meal so that the food can be digested quietly. (Almost every member of the animal kingdom except man does this, and animals don't get ulcers!)
>
> Try to live a calm, tension-free life — if you can't, you're probably in the wrong job!

It is better to avoid indigestion and stomach troubles than to have them to cure.

Influenza:

Influenza is a fever due to infection by a virus, and usually occurs in epidemics. It is not to be confused with the mildly feverish cold which today is so often wrongly referred to as 'Flu'.

True influenza has a very rapid onset, with high fever, shiveriness, headache, joint and muscle pains, **but not necessarily any 'cold' symptoms or cough.** It is a severe illness in the elderly or debilitated, and although it very often runs a rapid course in others, the convalescence is likely to be fairly prolonged; one of the diagnostic features of influenza is the sometimes marked depression and lassitude which follows it. Being a virus infection, antibiotics will have no effect at all on it, though antibiotics are sometimes given to reduce the possibility of an added secondary bacillary infection.

Treatment: the most effective drug in the treatment of influenza is still aspirin or a related product, taken in an adult dose of 2 tablets every 4 hours (except, of course, in the case of true allergy to aspirin), together with complete bed rest, light diet and plenty of fluids; the symptoms will generally resolve rapidly; should the temperature not be settling within 48-56 hours, then the diagnosis should be reconsidered.

Insect Bites:

Some people seem to be more prone to insect bites than others — mosquitoes of the Culex family appear to prefer the female sex (insects DO have intelligence!)

If you are one of those unfortunate people who suffer abnormally from insect bites, it will be worth your while to supply yourself with a good insect-repellant cream, of which there are many kinds on the market, and possibly also a supply of anti-histamine tablets such as Benadryl or Piriton which will reduce the irritation of Multiple bites. Local applications of Calamine, Caladryl or other similar lotions will also help.

Malaria:

Malaria is a disease of the tropics and subtropics occurring in this belt round the world; the further north or south of the Equator you go, the less malaria you are likely to encounter. Although it has been eradicated from many countries, it is still a disease of enormous importance, and as many as 5 million new cases occur each year.

There are four main types of malaria, each resulting from infection with one of the four different species of parasite, the parasites being known as Plasmodia; these parasites are carried by the female Anopheles mosquito (see page 69). The varieties of the disease are as follows:

	Type of Malaria	Parasite	Geographical Area	Relapses for
1	Malignant Tertian	P. Falciparum	Tropics	up to 3 years
2	Benign Tertian	P. Vivax	Subtropics	1 year
	Benign Tertian	P. Ovale	Tropics & Subtropics	short-lived
3	Quartan Malaria	P. Malariae	Tropics & Subtropics	several years

Of these diseases, Malignant Tertian ('MT') malaria is by far the most dangerous, often a 'Killer' disease if not treated.

Mode of Infection. The mature parasite is injected into the bloodstream of man by the bite of an infected Anopheles mosquito.

The parasite 'breeds' in man, developing up to a certain stage in his liver and then later in his blood, giving him malaria; this development stage takes 12 days — that is to say it takes 12 days from the bite before the parasite is liberated from the liver into the bloodstream, and it is this liberation in the bloodstream that gives the first attack of fever.

Another Anopheles mosquito bites the same man again, sucking up his now infected blood.

Further development of the parasites occur within the second mosquito, bringing them to maturity, and this mosquito will then bite another man giving him malaria.

Immunity: If local people are repeatedly bitten by infected mosquitoes, they gradually develop an immunity and the disease tends to diminish in severity until it dies out clinically and they remain more or less free from symptoms.

However, if the exposure to bites is short — i.e. a short malaria season, or a casual visitor — then the immunity dies out or does not have a chance to develop, as a result of which symptoms are liable to be severe.

A Typical Attack in the first case occurs in three distinct phases:

1. Feeling of coldness; shivering, temperature raised above the normal of 36.9°C (98.4°F).

2. Feeling of heat after about 1 hour; this lasts about 1½-3 hours.

3. Profuse sweating, then temperature drops.

However, this characteristic type of attack is not often seen except in cases in the very early stage of the disease, as the development of immunity gradually changes the whole nature of the disease.

After many attacks, the spleen and liver will become enlarged, and in MT malaria jaundice may develop.

Eventually, the paroxysms will come to an end and the whole disease quietens down; if not re-infected, relapses will occur at varying intervals, the relapses being less severe than the original attack.

Diagnosis of malaria should never be made unless the parasite has been unmistakenly demonstrated in the blood under a microscope by an expert.

Treatment: It is important NOT to **cure** a patient who has lived in a malarial area for a long time and will continue to do so; this is because, by curing him, the natural immunity which he has developed will be lost, and he will then suffer more with the severer primary attacks when — as he is bound to — he becomes reinfected.

Once again, it must be realised that treatment of malaria is a matter for skilled medicine if it is to be effective. The correct dosage of the most suitable type of anti-malarial for the specific disease being treated must be given, and this is a subject far beyond the scope of this book; however, we must consider the subject of suppressives.

A malarial **Suppressive** should be obligatory for a susceptible person moving into a known or suspected malarial district. By taking this in the correct manner, malaria will be 'prevented' - i.e. 'suppressed'. Examples of suppressives are:

Name of Drug	Adult Dosage
Amodiaquine (e.g. CAMOQUIN)	400 mgm (2 tablets) weekly.
Chloroquin	300-600 mgm (2-4 tablets) weekly
Pyrimethamine (e.g. DARAPRIM)	25-50 mgm (1-2 tablets) weekly.
Proguanil (e.g. PALUDRIN)	100-200 mgm (1-2 tablets) daily.

(Note: In some areas, parasites are resistant to these drugs.)

There are many other forms of suppressives besides these, informed medical opinion should be sought as to which is the best for the area you will be in. Whichever suppressive is selected, you should start taking it in the correct dosage **before** you enter the infected area, and continue for four weeks after you have left it.

Other preventive measures:

Sleeping quarters should be thoroughly sprayed with a reliable insecticide at dusk, as mosquitoes generally bite during the night.

In a known infected area, mosquito-netting should be used. The inside walls of permanent rooms should be coated with a residual contact insecticide (see Pages 127-8) as, after biting, the Anopheles likes to have a rest on these walls, and if this is done throughout all the buildings in the area, then you have gone a long way towards the control of the disease in this area.

Poisoning:

If you can remember just three rules of treatment, you will be able to cope reasonably with nearly all cases of poisoning:

1.   **Artificial Respiration** if the victim is not breathing, or is breathing poorly (see page 112).

2.   **Induce Vomiting** by pushing your fingers to the back of his throat, so that he will get rid of as much as possible of the poison that is still in his stomach. The only time that this does not apply is in the case of poisoning by a corrosive — strong acid or alkali; in such cases you will most likely see the burn marks on and around the mouth, and if you make him vomit, the corrosive will burn him again on the way up, and his burned stomach may easily rupture with the effort of vomiting. Give **Milk** to all cases of poisoning; if milk is not available, water will help by diluting any poison left in the stomach after vomiting has been induced.

3.   **Treat Shock** — see page 107.

Rabies:

There are many dogs and members of the dog family in desert areas and in neighbouring towns, and many visitors to these areas are rather concerned over the question of rabies, so this brief note on the subject is included.

Rabies is a disease due to a virus, usually transmitted in the saliva of the infected animal — dog, cat, wolf, jackal, fox, bat, squirrel, skunk, muskrat — in fact, almost any warm-blooded animal. The rabid animal **looks** ill, is savage and often is salivating more than usual. Most healthy dogs will bite only when they are provoked, or when **they feel they are provoked** — e.g. trespassing on what they see as their territory, teasing them, or threatening their food supply. A rabid dog, however, will bite even when unprovoked, so for preliminary diagnostic purposes it is important to think very carefully about the circumstances of the bite — specially from the viewpoint of the dog!

The disease in man is generally fatal; if symptoms developed, death used to be inevitable, but this is no longer necessarily the case.

There is **usually** a history of a bite by a dog, cat, or other warm-blooded animal; after an incubation period of anything from 10 days to 3 months the symptoms develop, starting with a feeling of acute anxiety followed by a change in sensation at the site of the bite, severe headache, excitement, fever, aversion to water, distressed breathing and finally paralysis and usually death.

Management and Treatment:

Once the symptoms of rabies have developed in man, the outlook is extremely grave; at present, not too much can be done in the way of therapeutic treatment, although at the time of writing (March 1980) there are reports that a new serum against rabies has been developed from the plasma of people innoculated against it. If this — or indeed any vaccine — proves to be effective against this very dreadful disease, it will be a real blessing.

Meanwhile, correct prophylactic treatment after a suspect bite offers a great deal of hope; to be of use, this treatment must be given as soon after the bite as possible.

Note:

1. Any bite by a stray dog, or by any of the animals mentioned above, must be regarded with suspicion.

2. Any UNPROVOKED bite must be regarded with even more suspicion.

If you have been bitten by a suspect animal, or under circumstances which make you believe that the animal may be rabid, then **do not kill it;** the animal should be kept locked up for 10 days; if it is still alive after 10 days, then it has not got rabies — and neither have you! However, in the event of the animal dying or being killed, the head should be cut off, packed in ice and sent by the quickest route to the nearest Pathology laboratory, with a full written description of all the circumstances.

Immediately you have been bitten, wash (do NOT scrub) the bite thoroughly with copious soap and water; by doing this you will eliminate most of the highly dangerous saliva. If you are very far from medical aid, and you are almost certain that the animal was rabid, then cauterise the bite as well as you can, using concentrated acid if you have any, or even a red-hot wire — painful, but not so unpleasant as the possibility of death from rabies.

Remember, the **saliva** from a rabid animal can be lethal, so be extremely careful to avoid getting any into small cuts or scratches — such as by allowing a suspect animal to lick any scratch, cut or break in your skin surface.

Sore Throat:

a. **Without Fever and/or Swollen, Painful Neck Glands:** Dequadin Lozenges should be sucked, 4-5 per day; these are usually very effective against the mild sore throat, as are also frequent hot mouth-washes or gargles with hot water to which a little salt or Bicarbonate of Soda has been added.

b. **With Fever and/or Swollen, Painful Neck Glands:** Take oral penicillin if available (see page 125).

Sunburn:

See page 79.

Toothache:

If you have severe toothache you are in for a pretty miserable time! But luckily there are one or two things you can do to help. Obviously you will have tried pain-relieving tablets, but if the toothache is severe enough to prevent you sleeping, then extra pillows to raise your head will ease the throbbing — in fact, the more vertically you can arrange yourself, the more likely you are to sleep!

If you can find a cavity in the aching tooth then you will get almost immediate relief by packing the cavity with a temporary filling made from a paste of zinc oxide powder and oil of cloves. (Ideally, if your trip was intended to be a lengthy one, you should have been for a dental check-up before leaving home.)

7   Snakes, Scorpions and Spiders

Snakes and Snake-bite:

The fear of snakes is deep-rooted in both civilised and primitive man, and not without reason, as there are still about 30,000 deaths from snake-bite each year throughout the world. However, when this figure is compared to the total number of recorded cases of snake-bite, the deaths resulting are seen to be only a fraction. **The great majority of people bitten by snakes recover completely,** in spite of the rather sensational stories one hears; but this does not mean that snake-bite is a condition which can be taken too lightly — prompt knowledgeable action will do much to reduce the risks.

The most important types of snakes belong to one of the 4 main groups:

1.   Vipers

2.   Cobras

3.   Tree Snakes (Pit Snakes)

4.   Sea Snakes

It is with **vipers** that we are mostly concerned in the desert, and for specific treatment it is important to learn the types of snake most prevalent in the area; if medical aid is available it is important either to take the snake itself with you if you can, or at least observe it enough to be able to sketch its main characteristics so that it may be positively identified and the correct anti-venom administered.

The poisonous effects of snake-bite are either **Local** or **General.**

Local effects are those at the bitten site and its immediate surroundings, and consist of —

Pain

Redness

Increasing swelling

Puncture wounds due to fangs

These signs are usually to be found on the lower leg or fore-arm, the areas most commonly bitten; the bites themselves are particularly prone to become infected.

General effects are the result of the absorbtion of the venom from the bite into the system, affecting either (1) the **Nervous System**, causing paralysis, interference with breathing, nausea, vomiting and sweating, or (2) the **Blood**, causing interference with the clotting mechanism, this interference usually being in two phases: firstly an increased bleeding tendency, followed by an increased clotting tendency. The venom of Vipers attacks the blood, whereas that of Cobras attacks the nervous system; thus if you are bitten by a snake in the desert, it is most likely to result in blood disorders. Nowadays, doctors usually give heparin or one of the other anti-coagulants for this kind of bite if anti-venom is not available.

Treatment. Remember, once it is injected, the venom will be absorbed into the circulation very rapidly indeed, so speed of action is essential, and you should waste no time in following these recommendations:

1. **Tourniquet.** Make a tourniquet as described on page 111 and apply at once as tightly as you can, round the thigh or upper arm according to whether the bite is in the upper or lower limb. (The tourniquet must, obviously, be applied between the bite and the trunk of the body.) Every 15 minutes the tourniquet **must** be loosened for 1 minute, then re-applied, and you must keep on doing this for 1½ hours at least, watching the patient carefully all the time for development of local or general signs, but specially during the 1 minute periods.

2. **Immobilise.** Keeping the bitten part at rest cuts down the blood requirements for that part, so reduces the speed of absorbtion of the venom; therefore immobilise the affected part. If the bite is in the upper limb, put the arm in a sling; if it is in the lower limb, then the patient must be kept lying down and not allowed to walk.

3. **Local Suction.** Local suction to the bite in order to suck out as much of the venom as possible must be done within seconds to be of any use. Make sure first that you have no cuts in your own mouth or the venom will be absorbed into your own body; spit out at once, repeating the suction again. Do this several times.

4. **Local Cleaning.** Local washing of the bitten area with soap and water should be done as soon as possible.

5. **Keep Cold.** The affected part should be placed in ice if you have it, or even cold water; like immobilisation this reduces the speed of absorption of the venom and also reduces the pain and swelling.

6. **Seek medical aid** as soon as possible. If this is not available but you have access to penicillin and benadryl, give the adult patient 4 tablets of oral penicillin (ask him if he has any history of allergy to penicillin — if so, don't give it) and 4 capsules of 25mgm Benadryl (see page 89). Repeat 2 tablets of penicillin every 4 hours.

7. **Re-examine** frequently for signs of developing general effects, and if you can, make a point of **writing down** every half hour the following:

Pulse Rate

Respiration Rate

Colour of Skin

Amount of Sweating ('Nil', 'Mild', 'Profuse', 'Extreme' etc.)

Any symptoms of which the patient complains.

This information, if accurate, is of value to a medically trained person who may take over later.

NOTE: Current medical opinion is that the use of potassium permanganate and the practice of local incisions over the bite area are — in unskilled hands at least — likely to do more harm than good and should **not** be employed.

Remember, THE OUTLOOK IN CASES OF SNAKE-BITE IS ALWAYS GOOD, except in:

1. Very toxic cases (multiple bites, undue sensitivity)
2. Delay or absence of treatment
3. The very aged
4. The very young

Snake Anti-Venoms. Anti-Venoms against most snakes are available today; if you are worried about the possibility of snake-bite, you might consider taking local advice on these and on their availability in your chosen area. Anti-Venoms are either polyvalent (a mixture of anti-venoms against most of the common snakes in that area) or specific for each type of snake, the latter being more effective, if the snake is known.

The German firm of Behring produce a set containing a sterilised disposable plastic syringe, a tourniquet, 4 x 10cc ampoules of anti-venom and alcohol swabs, all packed securely in a moulded box measuring 20 x 15 x 5 cms. These sets are specific for the area, using polyvalent sera. Areas covered are: North Africa, Central Africa, Europe, Central America, South America, Near East and Middle East. The sets should be kept cool, but refrigeration is not essential. The Expiry Date on each set should be checked on purchase.

KM

Scorpions:

Many types of scorpion are to be found in desert areas and they can give an extremely painful and unpleasant sting, the venom affecting the nervous system primarily, rather like that of the cobra, but to a lesser extent. Painful though the stings are, they are not generally dangerous to life except to young children. You will often hear it said that the black scorpion is more dangerous than the white, or vice versa. This is not necessarily true, a more accurate gauge being the size of the scorpion and hence the **quantity** of its venom. One of the most dangerous, therefore, is the Androctonus Australis, found in the northern Sahara and having a length of about 12 cms. The more normal size of an adult scorpion is 6-9 cms long.

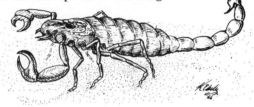

Scorpions are non-aggressive, nocturnal creatures which are rare in sand but common in stony desert. So beware when camping in such areas. (see Camp site, page 55). It is a wise precaution to look under any stones in your camp area before dark as it is underneath them that scorpions are most commonly to be found during the day, emerging at night.

Symptoms resulting from scorpion sting are intense pain at the site of the sting, redness and swelling; general symptoms may follow, these being increased production of sweat, saliva and tears; and possibly muscular cramps, fever and vomiting. The site of the sting is almost always in the foot or toes, rarely the hand. The scorpion stings by bringing its tail forward over its body, the paired poison glands being situated in the terminal segment of the tail.

Treatment. Once again, prompt local suction may be of value in removing some of the venom; packing the affected part in ice or immersing in cold water will help, as in cases of snake-bite. The patient should be treated for shock and if medical aid is available, scorpion anti-venom should be given. This is usually effective fairly rapidly in reducing the symptoms, and the severe local pain can be eased by injections of a local anaesthetic given by the doctor. Mortality in all cases needing — and receiving — treatment is less than 3%.

Spiders:

Very few spiders are dangerous to man, but the 'Black Widow' and the 'Tarantula' are both unpleasant enough to be worth considering.

The 'Black Widow', so called from her unpleasant habit of eating her 'husband' after mating, is to be found in Europe, N & S Africa, N & S America, Australia and New Zealand. Fully grown, she is about 1½ cms in length (3 cms including the legs). She has a black, shiny, rather bulbous body with a characteristic red mark on the abdominal surface — the so-called 'Hour-Glass' mark. Generally she is not aggressive and will bite only when she is cornered; the death rate from Black Widow bites is nothing like as high as popular belief would have it, being between 1% and 10% of all cases bitten. The effects of the bite, however, are not at all pleasant; these are:

1. Intense pain at the site of the bite.

2. Severe and very painful spasms of the muscles, specially the abdominal muscles; these 'cramps' may keep on recurring for as long as 3 days.

3. Shock is often severe, giving rise to the usual sweating, rapid pulse, restlessness and all its other symptoms.

Treatment: Treatment consists of pain relieving measures and treatment for shock; the spider should be preserved for identification if possible. If medical aid is available local anaesthetic should be injected into the bitten area, otherwise the treatment is primarily that of keeping the patient warm and as comfortable as possible with pain-relieving tablets; he should remain lying down until the symptoms have eased; if the spasms are severe, apprehension will be considerable, so reassurance is important.

The 'Tarantula' is a much larger spider (about 8 cm overall length) which is held in great dread by most people. However, this dread is more likely to be due to the rather terrifying appearance of the spider than to its danger. It is black, very hairy and is to be found for the most part in Southern Europe and North Africa.

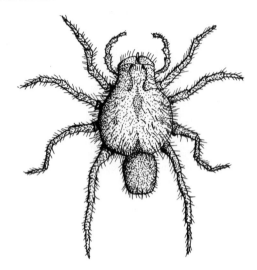

The Tarantula bite causes acute pain at the site of the bite, and very rarely can also cause a form of hysteria; seldom is it dangerous as the bite does not produce general symptoms; the only danger arises in the rare conditions where the patient is either in poor general health or allergic to the venom.

8 Immunization Against Specific Diseases

Before leaving your home country, find out from the local Public Health Authority which prophylactic inoculations are required by the Governments of the countries in which you are intending to travel. Apart from the obvious health protection that these will give you, being in possession of a valid and up-to-date 'Shot' Card will reduce preventable delays at ports and airports in countries where such inoculations are required. Be careful not to leave these until the last minute, as the validity of most of the inoculations does **not** start at the time of the injection, but several days later. For example, a Yellow Fever injection does not become valid until 10 days later, and Cholera 6 days.

Duration of the protection conferred following immunization varies according to the disease concerned:

Disease	Duration of Protection
Cholera	6 months
Typhoid	1 year
Typhus	1-2 years
Yellow Fever	10 years

Cholera

Cholera is a disease resulting from insanitary conditions; it is water- or milk-borne, and generally occurs in India, Pakistan, China, the East Mediterranean areas and Europe.

It affects the intestine, producing acute vomiting and diarrhoea, with death from dehydration in untreated cases.

Antibiotics are of extremely doubtful value in the treatment of cholera. However, modern transfusion techniques have reduced mortality to 15-30%, or less than 10% in a modern hospital.

Enteric Fever:

The enteric group of fevers consists of the following diseases:

1. Typhoid; world-wide distribution.
2. Paratyphoid A; occurs mainly in the East.
3. Paratyphoid B; occurs mainly in Europe.
4. Paratyphoid C; occurs mainly in Guyana.

They are all diseases which have a slow onset with fever, diarrhoea **or constipation**, and which usually respond rapidly to treatment with Chloramphenicol (Chloromycetin).

They also are generally diseases of insanitary conditions, often water-borne or milk-borne, and 'T.A.B.' immunization is an effective means of prevention, the letters 'T.A.B.' standing for Typhoid, paratyphoid **A** and paratyphoid **B**.

Of all the inoculations, this is the one which is probably most likely to give you a transient fever and a sore arm, so don't arrange any farewell parties for the two nights immediately following this inoculation!

Plague:

Inoculation against this disease is most useful if you are travelling to the Indian sub-continent, especially overland; it is also advisable for travellers to Ethiopia and Vietnam. Validity is for 6 months, and both local and general reactions can be severe.

Polio:

Poliomyelitis is a disease which is **less dangerous** in infancy than in adult life because paralysis is rare, and if it does develop, generally less severe.

The number of **local** adults developing polio in the tropics is relatively small owing to their high degree of naturally acquired immunity; but the incidence of polio among the non-immune, non-immunized travellers entering the tropics is high. So it is important for people entering the tropics. or even travelling anywhere away from their home country, to have had a course of polio immunization.

Smallpox:

On October 26th, 1977, a 23 year-old hospital cook, Ali Maow Maalin, survived an attack of smallpox in Somalia in the Horn of Africa. His was the world's last case of endemic smallpox —'he recovered, but smallpox died'. This was, and is, a remarkable and magnificent achievement by the World Health Organisation with international support, an achievement which to my mind did not receive anything like the acclaim it deserved — specially when one considers that smallpox has afflicted man for over 3,000 years and that even as late as 1963 — in spite of vaccination and reasonable control — it was still responsible for 25,000 deaths in that year alone. Since May 1978, the World Health Organisation has had on offer a reward of $(US) 1,000 for the first person reporting a confirmed case of endemic smallpox; I firmly believe that the reward will never be successfully claimed.

Some countries, however, still insist on smallpox vaccination, so you would be wise to check before starting your travels.

Tetanus (Lockjaw):

Tetanus is commoner in the tropics and sub-tropics than in Europe, South America or U.S.A., and it is important to be protected against it. Inoculation is frequently combined with the T.A.B. vaccine, and is then known as T.A.B.T.

Tetanus is a serious condition, resulting from infection by the tetanus bacillus in a deep, lacerated or punctured wound in which there is embedded dead material or dirt.

The toxin produced from the sporing bacilla affects the nerve-endings, eventually producing acute, generalised muscular cramps and spasms.

Long-acting immunity is conferred by inoculation with tetanus toxoid, but in cases where a suspicious wound exists in a non-immunized person, the tetanus anti-toxin is given (after a small test dose to make certain that the patient is not allergic to the anti-toxin), followed by a course of the toxoid at a later date.

Yellow Fever:

Yellow Fever is not found in deserts, but occurs mostly in South and Central America and in Africa south of the Sahara; it does not occur in Asia or the Orient, or in Australia.

It is due to a virus which attacks the liver; after an incubation period of 1-6 days, the classical symptoms develop; these are:

> Sudden onset of the disease, with elevated temperature and shivering.
> After 48 hours the fever drops but on the 4th day, jaundice, liver failure and heart disease may all occur.

Due to difficulties in storage of the vaccine, Yellow Fever inoculations must be administered at a recognised centre.

9 In the Last Resort....

I. Emergencies—Basic Principles of First Aid

(Note: This is intended to be only a guide to the fundamentals of First Aid, and is not meant to cover every contingency that might arise.)

1. **Don't Panic!** However bad and bloody the situation may appear to be, panic will undoubtedly make it much worse, and panic is one of the most infectious of all diseases.

2. **Remove Patient from Danger — Real or Threatening:** e.g. Fire, Petrol, Gas, Oil, Electric Cables, Machinery, — and do it as **gently as possible.** Make sure any electrical apparatus which may be in contact with the patient is turned off before you touch him.

3. **Apply Artificial Respiration if not Breathing** (see page 112).

4. **Stop Severe Bleeding:**-

   a. *From a limb:*
   DIRECT PRESSURE Pad and Bandage, applied firmly over the source of the bleeding. (Pad and Bandage can be made with clean, folded handkerchief and a tie or belt, if nothing else is available).

   ONLY if this is unsuccessful and bleeding is continuing, then apply a tourniquet VERY TIGHTLY, ABOVE the wound — that is, between the wound and the trunk of the body (see page 111) Release every 15 minutes for 1 minute; if fresh bleeding occurs, re-apply.

   b. *From Other External Sites:*
   Cover with Pad and Bandage, with moderate-to-strong pressure, according to the site of the wound.

   c. *From Internal Sites:* e.g. vomiting or coughing of blood. These are liable to be serious conditions requiring specialised treatment; the only First Aid is keeping the patient resting as quietly as possible, and treating him for shock.

   Get him to medical aid as soon as you can.

5. **Treat for Shock:**

   Warmth: Keep the severely injured man warm — put blankets above **and below** him, but **NO** hot-water bottles if he is unconscious or even drowsy, as he may easily receive severe burns on top of his other troubles. Remember, even in a hot climate, when you yourself may be sweating, the patient with shock will be cold and shivering; shock makes him cold; cold aggravates the shock, and so on until an irreversible state is reached and the patient dies. So - WARMTH IS VITAL.

   Reassure him as much as you can — an injured man is naturally worried about himself, and needs as much encouragement and reassurance as he can get.

   Give NOTHING to Eat or Drink until you are **quite certain** that he has no internal injuries, then plenty of warm, sweet drinks will help.

6. **If Unconscious,** then:

   Turn head to one side.

   Loosen any tight clothing around the neck.

   Make sure he has an unobstructed airway — i.e. clear out any debris from mouth and nose, and this includes any dentures or plates he may be wearing.

   If his face is flushed and there is no history of accident, (i.e. he has collapsed spontaneously) then prop him up; in in most cases, however, and certainly when his face is pale, then lie him down.

   NEVER, NEVER, NEVER, attempt to give an unconscious man anything to drink — you may drown him if you do!

   Do not leave him alone while he is still unconscious,

7. **Cover Wounds:** Apply a **clean** dressing — e.g. a clean folded handkerchief — and then LEAVE ALONE until such time as the wound can be properly and efficiently cleaned. Do NOT attempt to remove foreign bodies embedded in the wound. Generally, the less wounds are handled — and this includes burns and scalds — the better. If you attempt to clean wounds under non-sterile conditions you may easily introduce infection.

8. **Immobilize the Injured Part:** Movement of an injured part causes pain, and pain increases shock; therefore protect the injured part from movement as much as possible.

LEG : Splint, or strap, to other leg.

ARM : Place in a sling, or strap across the chest.

BACK : Place the patient on a rigid support — stretcher, plank, door, etc. — and do this by gently **rolling** him on to it, not by lifting, except in cases of suspected SPINAL INJURY which should be supported by feet and shoulders only - facing DOWNWARDS - while being lifted onto the support. However, any attempt at immobilization which is causing too much pain should be abandoned.

9. **Disposal:** Decide:

a. Whether the patient is a Walking, Sitting, or Stretcher case.

b. Whether he can be moved by Pick-up, Car, Ambulance, or needs a Plane.

c. The degree of urgency.

Having decided this, then contact the nearest Medical centre and explain — CLEARLY — how many cases there are, what sort and amount of transport you want and, if you are able, from what injuries they are suffering.

10. **A Note on Shock**

(It must be understood that the type of Shock we are considering here is what used to be known as 'Surgical Shock', and not the emotional type which one experiences on, for example, hearing bad news.)

Shock is a condition of collapse of the whole circulation due to sudden dilatation of internal blood-vessels following injury or haemorrhage. It varies in degree from being so mild as to be unnoticeable to being severe enough to cause death; in fact, it has been said that in the First World War more people died of shock than of the injuries which caused it.

Causes: Shock is due to:

a. Severe Bleeding
b. Severe Injuries, including burns.
c. A combination of both a & b.
d. Severe Pain - e.g. heart attack.

The greater the severity of any of those, the greater the resulting degree of shock.

Signs and Symptoms: Always look for these evidences of developing shock in all cases of injury or haemorrhage:

1. Faintness
2. Pallor of face and lips
3. Sweating, on a cold, pale, clammy skin
4. Feeble pulse, gradually becoming weaker and more rapid as the shock develops and the blood pressure falls
5. Possibly Vomiting
6. Possibly Unconsciousness

(Basically, these are also the signs of haemorrhage, visible or concealed; therefore if a patient who has not too much in the way of visible external injuries begins to show these symptoms, it means that he is becoming shocked and may well have some invisible internal bleeding. Early diagnosis of this condition can save time and lives, so it is important to keep taking the pulse at frequent intervals and noting it down, so that any changes will become apparent early, not when the patient suddenly collapses.)

Treatment: See Page 107.

11. **Poisoning:** See page 93.

II 'How To ....'

.... Take a Pulse.

This is usually taken at the wrist, though it may also be felt in other places, for example immediately in front of the ear. Remember that the radial (wrist) pulse is to be found on the front of the wrist about 2 cms (½-1 inch) above - i.e. towards the elbow - the root of the thumb, and it should be felt with the finger-tips, not the thumb.

Points which you should note when taking a pulse are:

1.   Rate per minute.
2.   Rhythm - Regular or irregular?
3.   Volume - Weak or strong?

Normal pulse rate is 72 per minute, but this is subject to great variation.

... Give an Intramuscular Injection (e.g. Snake Anti-Venom).

If the syringe to be used is not a sterilised disposable one, then it must be stripped down to its constituent parts and boiled - with the needle - for a full 10 minutes. Allow it to cool enough to be able to re-assemble (after washing your hands), then put the needle on, taking great care to touch the latter only by its base. Fill the syringe with the serum to be administered, hold it vertically and gently squirt out any air which has collected in the barrel; continue squirting till you are left with the correct dose in the syringe. Then sterilise the skin area by rubbing it with wool soaked in spirit. Holding the syringe like a dart, flick the needle in through the skin which should be stretched between a finger and thumb of the other hand; the needle should enter to a depth of about 2½ cms.

Before pressing the plunger, make sure that the point of the needle is **not** in an artery or vein by attempting to withdraw the plunger - if blood enters the barrel of the syringe then this indicates the point of the needle is in a blood vessel, in which case it would be dangerous to inject the serum; therefore withdraw the needle slightly and try to withdraw the plunger again.

The serum should generally be given by a slow and steady pressure of the plunger, rather than trying to push in too quickly. When the syringe is empty, withdraw it and rub the area firmly with a piece of cotton wool to disperse the serum.

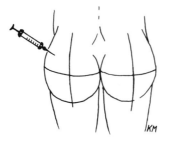

The safest and most painless site for giving an injection — specially a bulky one — is shown here and is the UPPER AND OUTER quadrant of either buttock. If you do not use this quadrant, there is a danger of hitting the sciatic nerve.

.... Use a Tourniquet.

A tourniquet must never be employed unless all other methods of attempting to control haemorrhage from a limb have failed, and even then certain rules MUST always be followed:

1. Make a note of the time applied.

2. Release FULLY every 15 minutes for 1 full minute, and carefully watch the wound area to see if fresh bleeding occurs; if it does, then re-apply for a further 15 minutes and so on.

3. Apply **very** tightly — if it is too loose this will tend to **increase** bleeding from a vein.

4. Apply the tourniquet ABOVE the wound — i.e. between the wound and the trunk.

Tourniquets may be made in various ways from different materials:

Rubber tubing, pulled **tight** and knotted over a handkerchief to prevent nipping the skin.

Handkerchief, folded diagonally into a strip about 4 cms wide; place round the limb, tie a half reef knot, lay a strong pencil, screwdriver, etc., over the knot, then complete the knot. Twist the pencil or screwdriver, using it as a 'turnkey', till the bleeding stops, then fix by tying down in position.

A strong necktie can be used in the same manner.

... Give Mouth-to-Mouth Artificial Respiration.

When it is necessary, it is very necessary! Artificial respiration must be performed as a matter of extreme urgency in a man who has stopped breathing, because if the oxygen content of the blood falls and the brain is deprived of its oxygen for longer than 3 minutes, irreversible damage to the brain tissue will almost certainly result.

IF IN DOUBT, DO IT!

1. Lie the patient flat on his back.
2. Make sure his mouth is clear of obstruction, e.g. dirt, dentures or sand.
3. Tilt his head right back so that he is facing vertically upwards, or even backwards.
4. Place your open mouth right over his, pinch his nostrils, and breathe out GENTLY, at the rate of 10-12 times per minute, watching his chest rise as you do so. (If it does not rise, there is some obstruction, so re-check the mouth and nose for obstruction; sometimes one short, sharp blowing respiration will be sufficient to clear an airway of mucus and enable the patient to breathe.)
5. Release the nostrils between each respiration.

... Give External Cardiac Massage.

This must be attempted whenever the heart ceases to function - i.e. whenever you cannot hear the heartbeat with your ear on the patient's chest, or feel a pulse.

1. Place the patient flat on his back.
2. Place the heel of one of your hands on the LOWER HALF of his sternum (breast bone).
3. Cover this hand with your other one.
4. AFTER EACH RESPIRATION, give 6-7 sharp and abrupt downward presses, at a rate of 1 per second.
5. Pause for the next respiration.
6. Repeat.

External Cardiac Massage must be carried out carefully as it can be dangerous if done incorrectly. It may be combined with mouth-to-mouth artificial respiration, given after each 6-7 pressures — possible with only one person, but better with two.

112

III. Calling off your Trip

Certain illnesses or injuries make it necessary for you to call off the trip and make efforts to reach skilled medical aid as soon as possible. Most of these, of course, are perfectly obvious; a few may be not quite so obvious.

A. Severe or persistent BLEEDING from any source

B. Severe or persistent CHEST PAIN

C. Severe or persistent ABDOMINAL PAIN

D. Persistent FEVER

E. Persistent VOMITING and/or DIARRHOEA which have not settled down with treatment

F. HEAT HYPERPYREXIA

G. UNCONSCIOUSNESS (other than diabetic, after it has been reversed with Glucagon)

H. Persistent SHORTNESS OF BREATH or DIFFICULTY IN BREATHING

I. INABILITY TO PASS URINE

J. CONVULSIONS

K. DISTURBANCE OF MENTAL STATE

L. SNAKE, SCORPION or SPIDER BITE with general symptoms

M. Persistent or recurring DISTURBANCE OF VISION

N. Persistent or recurring DISTURBANCE OF SPEECH

O. Any form of PARALYSIS — i.e. Motor (loss of movement) or Sensory (loss of sensation)

P. INJURIES giving rise to the following conditions:

   1. Severe or persistent bleeding from any source
   2. Presence of blood in urine after injury
   3. Increasing degree of shock
   4. Fractures of a large bone — obvious or suspected
   5. Penetrating wounds of chest or abdomen, skull or eye
   6. Continued shortness of breath
   7. Paralysis or persistent tingling of a limb
   8. Paralysis in any other area
   9. Inability to pass urine
   10. Any undiagnosed, persisting complaint after injury

FINALLY ...

When you come to your journey's end and arrive back home once more, triumphantly, or bloody-yet-unbowed, or on a stretcher, you will be in your own type of environment, and therefore may well be careless. Do remember that there are far more thieves in a city than in a desert, and a battered, travel-stained vehicle is a prime target for light fingered friends; do be doubly careful about security, otherwise you may find all your once-in-a-lifetime films, notes, and your expensive equipment, have been relegated to join the rest of your memories.

Memories DO fade; I would urge you most strongly to keep a daily record of some sort — it need not be anything more than a few words, but many years later, when sitting enfeebled in your wheel-chair, to be able to read 'George sat on by camel' will bring the whole scene flooding back to your ageing mind and you will cackle and wheeze with mirth, confirming the impression in the mind of your pretty but stay-at-home nurse that you always were a bit dotty, anyway!

Appendix A
Compass Errors

To use a compass to its maximum advantage in any vehicle, it is essential to understand the errors which affect the accuracy of the compass, since without such an understanding quite large deviations from the intended direction are easily possible.

Variation:

The first error is called Variation, and may be defined as the difference between the direction of **Magnetic** North and **True** North at the observer's position. (For example, in Libya this difference is very small and has little effect on navigation, whereas in nearby Morocco it is large enough to have to be taken into account.) All good charts mark this Variation on each sheet somewhere, but it is described in a variety of ways; the most usual, for example, is stated simply as 'Variation 10°W' or, another example, 'Variation 12°E'.

In the first example, this would mean that the Magnetic North, as indicated at the observer's position, would lie 10° to the West of True; like this:

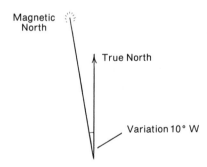

Now, it follows that if you lay off a course with a protractor on a chart using True North, and this course is 100° True --

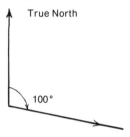

-- then, with 10°W Variation to consider, the magnetic course would be 110° Magnetic --

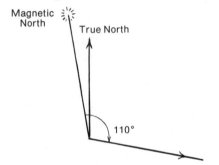

and, taking the second example of a Variation of 12°E, then the diagram would look like this:

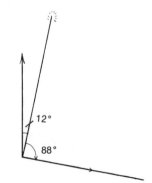

and the Magnetic course would be 088°.

A very simple way of remembering how to apply this is:

Variation East - Magnetic Least

Variation West - Magnetic Best (meaning 'largest')

Since Variation in Libya seldom exceeds 3°, it can be ignored here fairly safely, as mentioned earlier. However, in other countries, a 10° Variation, if ignored, would place you 10 miles out of position in a journey of 60 miles, which is obviously critical if you are heading for a rig or water-well in trackless desert.

Deviation:

The second error to be taken into account is Deviation. This may be defined as the difference between Magnetic North **indicated by the compass** and the **real** Magnetic North. This is more complex; to take a very simple example, let us assume that a vehicle has an aluminium (i.e. non-magnetic) chassis, wheels and bodywork. However, the engine, clutch and gearbox contain a fair proportion of iron and steel, the magnetic properties of which attract the north-seeking pole of a magnetic compass needle. Now, let us look at what happens to a compass mounted in the centre of a dashboard, when the vehicle is pointed along the four Cardinal points:

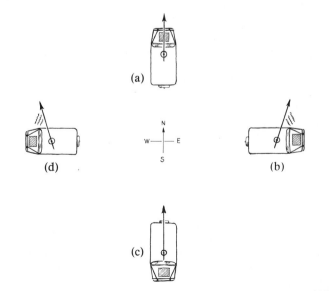

As you can see, with the vehicle heading North or South (a & c in the diagram), the attraction of the metal parts of the engine acts in line with the Earth's magnetic lines of force, and there is apparently no Deviation error on the compass. But, when the vehicle is heading East or West (diagram b & d) the compass needle is pulled off its North alignment by the engine and a deviation of (say) 10° creeps in.

This means that if you set out to reach a point 60 miles North of you in the vehicle, you would probably get there alright, even if you knew nothing about this error; but, if you set out to get to a place 60 miles East, you would end up, (if you did nothing but steer East by compass,) 10 miles South of your intended location.

Following this argument a little further, suppose you then (having not found your destination, and your tracks having disappeared) decide to go back to your starting point by steering 60 miles West, by compass. Instead of getting back, you would end up 22 miles South of your starting point. (A nice exercise in elementary geometry for you to check!)

Remember, the example given is only a very simple and basic one — Deviation can, in fact, be far more complex than this.

How to overcome the effects of this error? There are two ways; the first is to make out a correction card, which is precisely what is done in ships and aircraft. You do this by heading the vehicle on Magnetic North, using a hand-compass away from the vehicle and checking what the dashboard compass reads; then move the vehicle to a heading of 030° and repeat the procedure, and so on round to North once more. In the end, you have a card which looks like this:

FOR	STEER
360	001
030	028
060	055
090	080
120	116
etc.	etc.

However, I personally do not favour this; the perpetually changing metallic loads put into vehicles play havoc with your carefully worked out deviation card (a good friend of mine piled up a minesweeper during the war because the Captain's golf clubs were leaning against the compass!)

My own recommendation is to have a good hand-compass with you, and when you really need to navigate a vehicle by compass over featureless desert, the following procedure should be used:

a. work out the magnetic course from A to B, using the map and allowing for Variation (unless it is too small to matter).

b. stand well away from the magnetic influence of your vehicle and make an alignment with your hand compass along the course you wish to follow.

c. head your vehicle along this alignment; (you can now follow the Deviated heading indicated by the dashboard compass).

d. Repeat (b) & (c) EVERY TIME you have to alter your direction (e.g. skirting a sand dune) and/or certainly every ½ hour.

Note: Magnetic North has a regrettable tendency to move slightly each year. Good maps usually tell you by what amounts it alters, so this should be taken into account. The older map, the greater the adjustment which will have to be made.)

Appendix B
Water Filters

Katadyn

a   Pocket filter, (PF). Weight: 700g (1lb 9oz). Yield: ¾litre/min.

b   Various intermediate sizes; e.g. Stirrup Pump type, Type KFT. Weight: 5.3kg (11 lb. 11 oz.). Yield: 3 litres/minute.

c   Large filters, suitable for field stations, e.g. Type MF-31, made of stainless steel and containing 31 candles. Yield is up to 90 litres/minute. These filters have to be plumbed in to the water supply. All yield figures depend on the water pressure.

The life-span of the filter candles depends on the degree of contamination of the water to be filtered, and the filter will be regenerated by brushing the dirty surface; however, each brushing wears down the ceramic candles, and when the circumference has worn down to 125mm, then the candle must be replaced; if the candle is seen to be cracked, then it must be replaced immediately. I regret that I cannot be more accurate about candle life, but I have known new ones last as long as six months, and as little as six days — though the latter could well have been due to mis-handling.

Further information may be obtained from

> Katadyn Products Ltd.,
> CH-8304, WALLISELLEN,
> Industriestrasse 27,
> Switzerland.

> Tel: 01/830 3677

KFT

Safari.

'A' series filters: Flow rate — ½ gallon per minute (with hand, foot, or electric pump). Weight: 1.2kg. Cartridge life approx. 400 gallons.

'AB' series filters: Flow rate — 1 gallon per minute (with hand, foot, or electric pump). Weight: 1.5kg. Cartridge life approx. 800 gallons.

These filters can be obtained as either free-standing or bracket models. Further information on both types can be obtained from:

Steetley Chemicals Ltd.,
Safari (Water Treatments) Limited,
P.O. Box 56,
Basing View,
BASINGSTOKE, Hants.

Tel: 0256 - 29292

Appendix C
Suggested Food Supplies

1. Emergency Reserve

It is wise to be prepared for the worst and include in your rations approximately 3 days emergency food per person, to be packed away and to be used ONLY in emergency situations. Probably the best products in this field are the 'Total Diet' preparations which contain all the essentials of a balanced diet and are in powder form, needing only water to be added. They are useful when recovering from an illness, specially of a gastro-intestinal nature!

However, they do tend to deteriorate in high temperatures and so should be purchased in special export packaging, such as is supplied by Farley Health Products Ltd. for their 'Complan'. It is extremely important to maintain an adequate fluid intake, as you must remember that the water normally present in whole foods is, of course, not available in these powders.

You can complement this emergency reserve with such extras as canned 'ready meals', soups, etc., according to taste.

If you need to use any of this reserve, remember to restock at the earliest opportunity — there is no guarantee of only one emergency per expedition!

2. Supplies from Last Major Port of Call.

These should include all general supplies of 'processed' foods,
e.g.:

> Coffee and Tea
>
> Tinned or Powdered Milk
>
> Sugar, Salt, Pepper
>
> Glucose (e.g. Dextrasol tablets) (Glucose drink & salt tablet
> is a good combination for energy.)
>
> Cooking Oil
>
> Pasta, Rice, Porridge Oats
>
> Biscuits or Crackers
>
> Cheese (processed cheese does not keep well, canned
> cheese is probably better)
>
> Fruit Squashes, Dehydrated Instant Drinks
>
> Alcohol. Even if you are teetotal, a small supply of brandy
> or whisky can be very useful in an emergency situation.

Don't forget such things as can-openers, bottle openers,
matches, fuel for stoves, new torch batteries, etc.

3. Supplies en Route

Don't forget that you will be able to buy most of your fresh
supplies in local townships and villages, specially:

> Bread
>
> Fruit
>
> Vegetables
>
> Meat, Poultry, Eggs
>
> Lentils, Beans (both excellent sources of protein).
>
> Ground Nuts

Note: Raisins take up very little room and are a useful standby
with a high sugar content; Water-melons, Grapes and Tomatoes
are all very refreshing, tomatoes especially.   Dates are a very
good local buy (see page 49).

All local meat should be cooked well, and unless you know
otherwise, you would probably be wiser to treat it as stewing
meat.

Appendix D
Suggestion List — Medical Supplies

A. **Drugs & Medicines.**

Malaria Suppressive Tablets (see page 92).

Aspirin Tablets.

Paracetamol Tablets.

Sulphaguanidine Tablets for diarrhoea.

Dulcolax or Cascara Tablets for constipation.

Antacid (Indigestion) Tablets (Gelusil, Aludrox or Simeco).

Antibiotic Tablets - if you can get them. (e.g. Oral Penicillin, 200,000 units). Note: if you have to take an antibiotic, it is important that you take a full course — not less than 16 tablets, 1 every 4 hours.

Tyrozets or Dequadin Throat Lozenges.

2 or 3 Tubes of Penicillin or Terramycin Ointment.

Large Tube of Badional Gel, for burns (not available in U.K.).

Tube of Terramycin Eye Ointment.

Albucid Eye Drops.

Optrex Eye Wash.

Marzine, Dramamine or Avomine Tablets for travel-sickness.

Multi-Vitamin Tablets.

Cough Linctus.

1% Ephedrine Nose Drops or Spray.

Tineafax Ointment and Powder.

Salt Tablets - preferably NOT enteric-coated.

Benadryl Capsules, mgm 25.

Glucagon Set if a diabetic on insulin is in your party.

Analgesic Sprays, as used by sports trainers.

Any specific medicines upon which you are personally dependant.

Small quantities of Oil of Cloves and Zinc Oxide Powder for toothache (see page 95).

B. Dressings, etc.

Cotton Wool.

Sterilised Gauze Swabs - e.g. Mediswabs.

Surgical Lint.

Eye Pads.

Triangular Bandages.

7.5 cm Crepe Bandages.

Assorted Gauze Bandages.

Dettol.

Iodine or Merthiolate.

Surgical Spirit.

Hydrogen Peroxide, 12 Vol.

Elastoplast Adhesive Bandages.

Large Box of Bandaid Dressings.

2.5 & 5 cm. width rolls of Zinc Oxide Adhesive Strapping.

Skin-closure 'Suture' Strips e.g. Steri-strips.

C. Instruments.

Surgical Scissors.

1 pair Toothed 'Dissecting' Forceps.

1 pair Untoothed 'Dissecting' Forceps.

Safety Pins.

2 Clinical Thermometers. N.B. Keep these in a **cool** place!

D. Miscellaneous

Halazone Tablets (e.g. Sterotabs, from Boots, or Puritabs) for water purification.

Insect Repellent Cream.

Caladryl Lotion for sunburn.

Anti-Snake kit (see page 99).

Mosquito Netting.

Cotton Buds.

Extra pair of spectacles if you normally wear them.

1 copy of 'Stay Alive in the Desert'!

Appendix E
Insecticides

One of the main problems with modern insecticides is the relative ease and speed with which insects seem to be able to develop a resistance to them, which means that research into the whole field of insecticides is a continuing process. In recent years, there has been much concern (some of it very valid, some of it hysterical) about the effects of insecticides, directly and indirectly, on man, but I do not propose to attempt to deal with that thorny problem in this book.

By far the largest and most widely used group of insecticides is the group of 'Contact' poisons, though there are also 'Fumigants' and 'Repellants'.

Contact Insecticides

These are insecticides which act directly on the insect through external contact. There are two main varieties, 'Residual' and 'Non-Residual'.

1.   Non-Residual Contact Insecticides.

The main ingredient of these is Pyrethrum, which acts very rapidly and generally kills rapidly, though some of the larger insects may recover. Since pyrethrins as a group decompose in sunlight, they have a short effect and are therefore used as 'space-sprays' — for example, aerosols or 'flit'-guns. These insecticides are useful for disinfecting rooms, tents, vehicles including aircraft, but are not generally very effective if used out of doors. They should **never** be used anywhere near uncovered food.

2.   Residual Contact Insecticides.

These insecticides are resistant to sunlight and therefore are much more stable, one application remaining effective for many months; they are absorbed through the foot-pads of insects alighting on a surface coated with them, and progress to the central nervous system, causing paralysis and death after a few hours.

The largest group of the residual contact insecticides is known as the 'chlorinated hydrocarbons', although many other groups are being developed at present and may eventually supersede these. The three chlorinated hydrocarbons which are most in use today are:

1. D.D.T. (Dichloro-diphenyl-trichloroethane).

2. Gamma-BHC ('Gammexane' and 'Lindane').

3. Dieldrin.

The last two, however, are held by many to be unsafe, and resistance to both of them is becoming marked. In some countries even DDT has been banned.

Another group under recent investigation and development is the 'organo-phosphate' range, which includes D.D.V.P. and Malathion, while the even newer Permethrin (a stable pyrethroid) is giving rise to great optimism.

Control of Specific Insects by Insecticides

(It must not be forgotten that there are many methods of control of insects other than by insecticides, such as: general hygiene, good sanitation, fly-screening, elimination of breeding places; in other words, don't forget the basics when trying to reduce the insect nuisance. In all cases, therefore, control should be aimed primarily at destroying the breeding grounds, by burning, 'digging in' then finally by insecticidal spraying. The basic principle, of course, is that there is little use in killing the adult insects while allowing breeding to continue at a much greater rate in an unnoticed garbage dump or stagnant pool; once the breeding areas have been dealt with, then you can go after the adults).

Fleas:
Treat ADULTS with Dieldrin or DDT.
CLOTHING, BEDDING and FLOORS should be dusted with 2% Dieldrin or 10% DDT powder.

Houseflies:
Treat ADULTS with Pyrethrins (Aerosol Sprays).
Treat BREEDING GROUNDS with Malathion Sprays; add Paradichlorobenzene to garbage cans — 60 gms per bin per week.

Mosquitoes:

(a) Anophelines:
Treatment of BREEDING GROUNDS needs to be undertaken on a scale larger than is covered by this book. For large camps in a known malarial region, expert advice should be sought. Residual spraying of INTERIOR WALLS should be with either (1) DDT, 2 gms per sq. metre; or (2) Dieldrin, 0.5 gms per sq. metre. (Both these remain effective for 6 months.)

(b) Culicines:
Treat all small water-pools and other BREEDING PLACES — usually near habitation — with 2% solution of DDT in Ethyl Alcohol. This is sufficient to kill all LARVAE for 6 weeks.
ADULTS should be controlled with residual spraying, as for Anophelines.

Sandflies:
ADULTS are difficult to locate.
Spray BREEDING GROUNDS with DDT, BHC or Dieldrin Residual sprays.

Simulium Flies:
Treat LARVAE with 1 part DDT per 10 million parts water.

Bedbugs:
Ordinary HOUSE-spraying with DDT and/or Pyrethrins, special attention being paid to cracks in walls and floors, and to BEDS and BEDCLOTHES; repeat at 10-day intervals. Fumigation of rooms and bedding with sulphur candles also helps.

Cockroaches:
Treat usual 'RUNS' with BHC powder, or use aerosol sprays of pyrethrins and piperonyl butoxide.

Lice:
10% DDT Dust, applied to CLOTHING.
HEAD LOUSE; 6% DDT with added Benzyl Benzoate in lotion form.
Note however that resistance by lice to DDT seems to be increasing, and research to find effective substitutes is continuing.

Mites (Scabies):
Scrub the WHOLE BODY with soap and water; apply Benzyl Benzoate or Tetmosol 5% to the whole body except the face and allow to dry. (Note: Benzyl Benzoate may irritate some skins).
Tetmosol soap may be useful as a prophylactic.

Scorpions:

Apply Gamma-BHC or 10% Malathion to inside and outside WALLS of houses by means of a spray, also to likely scorpion areas — e.g. stony ground, stacked camping materials, etc.

Ticks:

Spray VEGETATION with Lindane wettable powder in aqueous suspension — recommended strength: 100-150 mgm per sq. metre.

Treat ANIMALS with 1% DDT washes or with 5-10% DDT Powder.

Appendix F
Sources of Information

Rather than give a list of suppliers and addresses, which will soon be out of date — and may not be relevant to the country in which you are reading this book — I would suggest that intending travellers make use of the many sources of information which are available virtually everywhere.

LIBRARIES, both local and national, usually hold up-to-date editions of trade directories, telephone 'yellow pages' and other useful lists. Libraries also have helpful staff, who generally welcome the chance to join in your 'quest' for addresses as a pleasant change from tracking down the latest whodunnit!

Most countries maintain TOURIST INFORMATION CENTRES in the capitals and major cities of the world. One of the main functions of these centres is to attract and advise intending travellers, and for this reason they have access to many sources of help and further information. They can give details of weather conditions, transport to and within the area concerned and other relevant travel information.

EMBASSIES or CONSULAR OFFICES will give passport and visa information, as well as details of the laws of the country, regulations concerning immunization, import and export of equipment, currency, foodstuffs, cost of living, etc. They will also advise on any areas out-of-bounds to foreigners (e.g. many parts of the U.S.S.R.).

TRADE DEPARTMENTS of Embassies: Many Arab countries operate a ban on products made by companies with Israeli connections. Enquiries will show which firms are involved — so avoid any of their equipment (which might be confiscated, and for which you would be unlikely to get spares or service).

National GEOGRAPHICAL SOCIETIES or Explorers Clubs. Returned travellers are often eager to share their experiences, and may well have written about them.

CAR MANUFACTURERS and IMPORTERS may have useful information on specialised vehicles or optional equipment.

MOTORING ORGANISATIONS will be able to advise on driving permits, insurance requirements, speed restrictions, traffic regulations, etc.

The local branch of your MINISTRY OF HEALTH or local HEALTH AUTHORITY will advise you on health requirements and will be able to refer you to an inoculation centre for the necessary 'jabs' and certificates.

(Don't forget, if you are going to be away for any length of time, to make enquiries about how such absence may effect your social security status on return.)

BANKS can be useful sources of fiscal information — currency restrictions, letters of credit, emergency transfer of funds, etc.

CAMPING CLUBS and magazines will be mines of useful information about suppliers and addresses.

Specialist SHOPS will often be able to supply catalogues of interesting equipment. Two I have found very useful being

1. Alexander Motor Accessories,
   Alexander Engineering Co. Ltd., Haddenham, near Aylesbury, Bucks.
2. Black & Edgington (Sidcup) Ltd. Tropical Catalogue, Murray House, Murray Road, Orpington, Kent, BR5 3QY

This should be enough to start the hunt. Never fail to follow up a lead. Tracking down the latest piece of specialized desert camping equipment can often be like a treasure hunt — one clue leads to another. Do explore every avenue that opens up — you may not find what you are looking for, but who knows what you may find instead!

Finally, it is well worth while checking with your own FOREIGN OFFICE or MINISTRY OF FOREIGN AFFAIRS — they have a vested interest in making sure that you don't get into any potentially dangerous situations, especially political, or have problems of repatriation if things do go wrong.

On arrival in each foreign country, register with your own embassies or consulates — they can give the latest information on any trouble spots or changes in regulations. Also, let them know when you intend leaving the country — if trouble breaks, they do try to contact all their nationals, and you won't be popular if time has to be wasted trying to track you down long after you have returned home and are busy planning your next adventure — to the South Pole?

Appendix G

Weights, Measures and Equivalents

Conversion Tables

LENGTH centimetres	cm or inches	inches	WEIGHT kilogrammes	kg or pounds	pounds
2.54	1	0.39	0.45	1	2.21
5.08	2	0.79	0.91	2	4.41
7.62	3	1.18	1.36	3	**6.61**
10.16	4	1.58	1.81	4	8.82
12.70	5	1.97	2.27	5	11.02
15.24	6	2.36	2.72	6	13.23
17.78	7	2.76	3.18	7	15.43
20.32	8	3.15	3.63	8	17.64
22.86	9	3.54	4.08	9	19.84
25.40	10	3.94	4.54	10	22.05
50.80	20	7.87	9.07	20	44.09
76.20	30	11.81	13.61	30	66.14
101.6	40	15.75	18.14	40	88.19
127.0	50	19.68	22.68	50	110.2
152.4	60	23.62	27.22	60	132.3
177.8	70	27.56	31.75	70	154.3
203.2	80	31.50	36.29	80	176.4
228.6	90	35.43	40.82	90	198.4
254.0	100	39.37	45.36	100	220.5

DISTANCE kilometres	km or miles	miles	VOLUME litres	litres or gallons	gallons
1.61	1	0.62	4.55	1	0.22
3.22	2	1.24	9.09	2	0.44
4.83	3	1.86	13.64	3	0.66
6.44	4	2.49	18.18	4	0.88
8.05	5	3.11	22.73	5	1.10
9.66	6	3.73	27.28	6	1.32
11.27	7	4.35	31.82	7	1.54
12.88	8	4.97	36.37	8	1.76
14.48	9	5.59	40.91	9	1.98
16.09	10	6.21	45.46	10	2.20
32.19	20	12.43	90.92	20	4.40
48.28	30	18.64	136.4	30	6.60
64.37	40	24.86	181.8	40	8.80
80.47	50	31.07	227.3	50	11.00
96.56	60	37.28	272.8	60	13.20
112.7	70	43.50	318.2	70	15.40
128.7	80	49.71	363.7	80	17.60
144.8	90	55.92	409.1	90	19.80
160.9	100	62.14	454.6	100	22.00

Metric Measures and Equivalents

Length
1 millimetre (mm)		= 0.0394 in
1 centimetre (cm)	= 10 mm	= 0.3937 in
1 metre (m)	= 100 cm	= 1.0936 yds
1 kilometre (km)	= 1000 m	= 0.6214 mile

Surface or Area
1 sq cm (cm²)	= 100 mm²	= 0.1550 sq in
1 sq metre (m²)	= 10,000 cm²	= 1.1960 sq yds
1 are (a)	= 100 m²	= 119.60 sq yds
1 hectare (ha)	= 100 ares	= 2.4711 acres
1 sq km (km²)	= 100 hectares	= 0.3861 sq mile

Capacity
1 cu cm (cm³		= 0.0610 cu in
1 cu decimetre (dm³)	= 1000 cm³	= 0.0351 cu ft
1 cu metre (m³)	= 1000 dm³	= 1.3080 cu yds
1 litre (l)	= 1 dm³	= 0.2200 gallon
1 hectolitre (hl)	= 100 litres	= 2.7497 bushels

Weight
1 milligramme (mg)		= 0.0154 grain
1 gramme (g)	= 1000 mg	= 0.0353 oz
1 kilogramme (kg)	= 1000 g	= 2.2046 lb
1 tonne (t)	= 1000 kg	= 0.9842 ton

British Measures and Equivalents

Length
1 inch		= 2.54 cm
1 foot	= 12 inches	= 0.3048 m
1 yard	= 3 feet	= 0.9144 m
1 rod	= 5.5 yards	= 5.0292 m
1 chain	= 22 yards	= 20.117 m
1 furlong	= 220 yards	= 201.17 m
1 mile	= 1760 yards	= 1.6093 km
1 nautical mile	= 6080 feet	= 1.8532 km

Surface of Area
1 sq inch		= 6.4516 cm³
1 sq foot	= 144 sq inches	= 0.0929 m²
1 sq yard	= 9 sq feet	= 0.8361 m²
1 acre	= 4840 sq yards	= 4046.9 m²
1 sq mile	= 640 acres	= 259.0 hectares

Weight
Avoirdupois
1 ounce	= 437.5 grains	= 28.350 g
1 pound	= 16 ounces	= 0.4536 kg
1 stone	= 14 pounds	= 6.3503 kg
1 hundredweight	= 112 pounds	= 50.802 kg
1 ton	= 20 cwt	= 1.0161 tonnes

Capacity

1 cu inch		= 16.387 cm³
1 cu foot	= 1728 cu inches	= 0.0283 m³
1 cu yard	= 27 cu feet	= 0.7646 m³
1 pint	= 4 gills	= 0.5683 litres
1 quart	= 2 pints	= 1.1365 litres
1 gallon	= 8 pints	= 4.5461 litres
1 bushel	= 8 gallons	= 36.369 litres
Apothecaries		
1 fluid ounce	= 8 fl drachms	= 28.413 cm³
1 pint	= 20 fl ounces	= 568.26 cm³

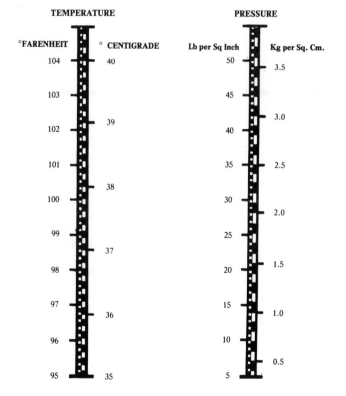

TEMPERATURE

°FARENHEIT   ° CENTIGRADE

PRESSURE

Lb per Sq Inch   Kg per Sq. Cm.

Bibliography.

I gratefully acknowledge the references I have made to the following works during the writing of this book:

'Tropical Diseases' (15th Edition) by Sir Philip Manson-Bahr.

'Tropical Diseases' by Sir Alexander Biggam and Frederick J. Wright.

'Insecticides' and 'Anti-Malarial Drugs', Bulletins 1 & 2 of the Ross Institute, London.

'An Introduction to Parasitology' by John M. Watson, D.Sc(Lon), A.R.Sc.

'Notes on the Preservation of Personal Health in Warm Climates' published by the Ross Institute, London.

'Libye, Royaume des Sables' by Freddy Tondeur.

'Survival' (Dept. of the Air Force)(U.S. Air Force).

'Safe Outback Travel' (1st Edition) by Jack Absalom.

'The Travellers' Health Guide' by Dr. Anthony C. Turner.

'World Health' Magazine (W.H.O.) Bulletins.

'Encyclopaedia Britannica'.

'Nature is your Guide' by Harold Gatty.

'The Great Sahara' by James Wellard.

Acknowledgements.

I would also like to express my gratitude to all the countless friends who have given freely their advice and help — pilots, engineers, mechanics and many others engaged in all branches of work in the desert; to the Bechtel Corporation for permission to reproduce the photographs on Pp 29 and 60; to Doug Niven (Cars) Ltd.; to the Overseas Group of Dunlop Ltd; to Henry Brown; to Rosario Casella without whose imagination and help the first edition of this book would never have seen the light of day; to Capt. John Huckle for the section on compass errors; to Professor Bradley of the Ross Institute for allowing me the use of the Institute Library; to Roger Lascelles for his help, encouragement and patience with my dilatoriness in getting down to the second edition; and finally and traditionally to my wife, without whose help in typing the manuscript, many suggestions and interminable nagging you would certainly not be reading any of these words now.

K.E.M.M.